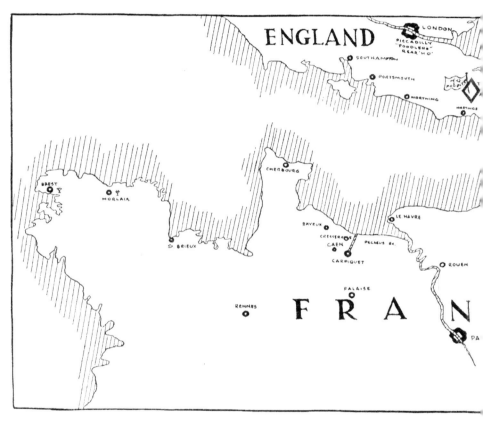

ENGLAND

LONDON
PICCADILLY
"POODLEGS"
REAR'HO'

SOUTHAMPTON

PORTSMOUTH

WORTHING

HASTINGS

CHERBOURG

BREST

MORLAIX

LE HAVRE

BAYEUX

CRESSERONS

CAEN

PELMEUS DR.

ST BRIEUX

CARPIQUET

ROUEN

RENNES

FALAISE

F R A N

PA

THE PLA

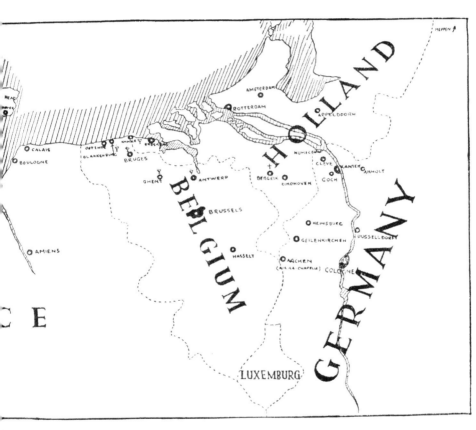

'PLAYBOYS'

B Squadron 141 RAC (The Buffs) 1944–45

The Naval & Military Press Ltd

Published by

The Naval & Military Press Ltd

Unit 5 Riverside, Brambleside
Bellbrook Industrial Estate
Uckfield, East Sussex
TN22 1QQ England

Tel: +44 (0)1825 749494

www.naval-military-press.com
www.nmarchive.com

Printed and bound by CPI Group (UK) Ltd, Croydon, CR0 4YY

*In reprinting in facsimile from the original, any imperfections are inevitably reproduced
and the quality may fall short of modern type and cartographic standards.*

This is not an "OFFICIAL" history.
It is merely a private memento to
remind you of the days spent with
"B" Squadron 141 R.A.C. (The Buffs)
in those momentous days of the
France -- Germany Campaign
1944   1945.

STATUS QUO ANTE

"B" Squadron always did defy the simple adjectival phrase. Within the regiment each Squadron will inevitably acquire its own particular quiddity. The chance conjunction of officers, N.C.O's and men (civilians in the main)—selected willynilly, thrown headlong together in the melting pot of training and events. Out of this will come the synthesis, the new identity which is neither Whittingham nor Bremner, neither SSM Cole nor Tpr. Pitt but something of them all. With 'B' Squadron there just wasn't any descriptive label you could tie to this except—well, 'B' Squadron. The nearest ever reached perhaps was a title earned during a hectic month amongst the delights of Antwerp, whilst the remainder of the regiment wandered homeless in Holland. Peeved by the comparative dullness of life in the Low Countries a regimental wit made slighting comment on "The Playboys". All unwitting he provided to every man in 'B' Squadron the appelation which they liked. It was "just the job."

Thenceforth pennants embroidered with all the insignia of Mayfair floated from wireless masts, here and there a pannier door displayed the same in paint, and real silk hats adorned the projecting parts on every tank. It was the spirit of "Playboys" which took them laughingly through hell and high water—and from then on the devil looked after his own, taking them safely where angels feared to tread.

It was the custom of that great Scottish personality, Lt-Col. Waddell, to drive his jeep in long night journeys from one end of the bridgehead to the other, from Squadron to Squadron and battle to battle. After a long pensive silence during such a nomadic wandering he removed his pipe, swung the wheel hard over to avoid a shell hole, as usual hit it nevertheless full tilt and remarked to his passenger, "What ah like about 'B' Squadron is that when they make a ballsup they doan't try to make excuses

1

—they laaf and bounce back. And its the same when they hit trouble—they doan't whine. They're a robust Squadron—aye, that the worrd, robust.''

Outstanding in the moulding of 'B' Squadron was Major Bremner, the "Mad Von", who had the Squadron first as an infantry company and after its conversion until the Spring of 1943, when he voluntarily left as he put it "for a date with his son in the Middle East". With his impressive aide, SSM Cole, he moulded into his Squadron a soldierly discipline of the finest sort. The discipline that becomes an attitude and a second nature—neither the slick line of bull wherewith to take in senior officers nor the mere compliance with orders as and when they appear. It is said that on one day an old offender was to be brought up before him. SSM Cole flung open the office door and in his stentorian tones began the complicated business of manoeuvring the soldier in front of the Von's desk. "Tpr Snooks—Tension—Left Turn—Quick March—Left, Right, Left, Right, Left Wheel—." But before ever he got there out of the mouth of Homer came the words, "Well Snooks I know you and you know me—seven days C.B.", and without halt SSM Cole carried on with the equally complicated business of marching him out. Major Bremner was a martinet—but a just one. Human too—"Well Pheasant I'm poodling myself this week"—thereby becoming unawares O.C. Poodlers Club. Above everything he was a soldier, for all that he was a civilian. And the same spirit was carried on later by Major Spearpoint and Major Ryle. It was this soundness of character, this unassuming toughness, which had much to do with the way in which 'B' Squadron met its early disasters in the field and came back smiling and asking for more.

This was the Squadron which landed in France on 22 June and proceeded to harbour at St. Gabriel. Sydney Spearpoint, a young married man of 28 from the Stock Exchange, was in command—dark haired, buccaneering type, tough as they make them, happy as a sandboy and well capable of quaffing an infinite number of pints. He was very ably seconded by Nigel Ryle, 29 and of extraordinary varied experience in Civvy Street. Proud of his trim moustache, proud of his military figure (he was one of the very few people capable of still looking like a soldier even in battle dress), he occasionally took time off to worry about his two grey hairs. Favourite pastime was the imbibing of large quantities of liquor at the bar, expatiating meanwhile with first hand knowledge on the evils of big business or the narrow-mindedness of married men who denied to their wives the simple pleasures of love-affairs with other men. Then wind up at closing time by walking off with some delightful piece in the corner on whom some other officer had been assiduously working the whole evening. A Squadron you might already hazard that drank a pretty beer. Third in the HQ Trio was Captain Moss (Bonko)—a hefty great chap with an enormous appetite, considerable "tank" knowledge and an extraordinary genius for improvisation. Recently married and only 25 he had been a metallurgist. He too on occasion would hold his own with any at the bottle. In a few days HQ was to be augmented by that most popular of all officers, Nippy Chips—the wee versatile witty Captain John Dean, regimental L.O.

Linked with HQ of course was SSM Boyes, a regular of absolutely sterling worth who spoke his Hampshire accent like a native born. "Speedy" was to take his echelon up to the tanks through bombing raids and mortar stonks, up "Down" routes and down "Up" routes—but he always got it there and never once were the "babies" unreplenished. "Oi got praaper bitched in that last town we came through sur—oi follows Diamond like you said, then on a sudden foinds oi'm on Heart. Course oi'm on the ten tonner with the echelon behind and we can't turn round no-hows. Still oi managed to get back on Diamond in the end sur". How nobody knows—but he'd done it. As it turned out he was destined one morning for even greater heights. In the sunny days of Normandy he had leisurely retired for the morning's luxury session at the Squadron's compo two-holer, not comparable perhaps with the finer products of Cpl Hare but passing fair and deeply dug. Some hygienic maestro however had earlier thought to make a modification unofficial and unpublished, to wit he had poured in some two gallons of petrol wherewith to cure the flies. Behold then Speedy, esconced at last to his liking, looking at the blue sky, leisurely lighting a cigarette then throwing the

3

match into the nearest receptacle—and in a split second he is airborne on an explosive flash. Fortunately he organised the perfect pancake landing and emerged cleaned, healed and triumphant from the hospital some weeks later—once more to defy the "No Entry" signs and subsequently to receive the MM.

With him that arch-conspirator and Prince of Scroungers SQMS Crouch—to his friends and Julie, 'Bill'. "Bill" well knew that a too strict regard of rules and regulations meant that men went hungry and went in rags—let us give praise and thanks to him and all his confreres in the Army who, faced not with diagrams nor figures but realities, dared to outwit the paper merchants in their remoter castles.

So far as officers go 'B' Squadron was predominantly bachelor and of all the Troop Commanders only one, Lt. Sander, was married. Mike Henderson, called up almost straight from Public School, had 6 Troop. On your first few encounters with him his quiet manner hid a most devastating wit and a nature so fine that it was second to none—philosophic, a Catholic who somewhat surprisingly adhered in practice to his principles yet in his superb tolerance well able to encourage others in their breach. A cricketer and the most mischievous sod out. Chief delight was to drink under the table someone who for perhaps a whole week had religiously drunk *him* under the table and put *him* to bed every night—then to sway over his victim chanting, exultant. Lieut Beck had 7 Troop and Lieut Brooke the original ill-fated 8 Troop. Pete Sander had 9 Troop. He too was of the cream and had a personality which was unique. Completely fearless talented, charming, a little exotic, he would go to great lengths to salve his conscience and as such was not a little susceptible to leg pulling. His abilities and the breadth of his liberal mind could however lead only to bitter frustration in the narrow confines of Army life. Lieut Mason had 10 Troop. Of the original nine officers three were to be killed, five wounded and one left the Squadron shortly after landing.

Then there were the Troop Sergeants—the backbone, the guys who had trained the Regiment as infantry, had trained it then in tanks and at last in those hectic months

4

before D day had trained it in Crocs. Popular "Jake" Morley—devil-may-care, pugnacious, ham handed, treating all things as he treated the slabs of butter in his civvy stores, just slapping them around. Sgt Wetherell—tall, bespectacled, austere looking, quiet, reliable. Sgt Maddock—slight build, intellectual, dynamic. Sgt Burton—garrulous, Cockney. Sgt. Decent with his tousled ginger hair—long and lean, fierce, tough as a millstone. "Pip" Pipkin—small dark mighty atom, a Regular who didn't care one damn for any officer or man, be he English or be he Hun. This was the order of their Troops.

And what of Ivan Ivanovitch? Not a man in the Squadron but does not deserve to be mentioned here if space only permitted. To a man they played the best game of their life, and some where killed, some were wounded and some happily survived. In a long line they spring to mind. That Man of Kent Sgt "Hardy" Norrington and Cockney Tpr "Johny" Stroud—these two, words cannot describe. We give them to you without comment as the real, the true, the finest sterling Englishmen. Sgt. Bob Little ("Oh my, poor guy—") and his fitters who kept the tracks rolling as no one else could—not in a back room garage either, but where the mortars crumped and the shells landed. Bateman, veritable tyrant of the air after Sgt Douse was wounded, keeping the Squadron way on net in action. Whittingham and Tuit—taking that old 15-cwt Water Truck on their own initiative anywhere and any time. Old "Dick Whittington" drove that old thing as if he were hugging the wheel of a Mercedes on Brooklands, and every tank crew knew that they would never go short of water if it rained mortars. We're rather proud of those two. Sgt Jack Huxtable—stolid and smiling as ever in the hottest places. McPherson—"Ye ken fine Underwood that yourr tank'll no go faster than mine." Davenport, operator, in slow Yorkshire tones, "Just found a new line in mines here, sir, shall I try and neutralise one--rather interesting I should think". The coolest man in creation. Sgt Gilbert, "Well sir I happen to have made provision for this sort of thing though it's strictly illegal and I've got a few extra gas bottles laid by. I rather though this sort of thing might happen". Cpl Denton, tank driver—conscientious, fatherly, idealist. Mills, gunner—"Lovely!".

5

Cpl Barrett—hard working wizard of tech stores. Mitchell, jeep driver—what don't we owe to that paragon of driving and ability ? A sense of direction like a dog's sense of smell. The unfailing ability to carry out any job—to give "Orders" to Troop Commanders, to round up tank columns, to rescue inebriates. Whatever it was it could safely be left to "Mitch." Or Elworthy, staff car driver, for that matter—steady, genial, capable. Those hard-working knowalls of Squadron affairs—Cpl Kessell and L/C Ruth. Yes. a long line of them—Staples, Hudson, Waters, Simpson, Snashall, Walsh, Cross, South American Joe. And a hundred others.

IF I SHOULD DIE

If any place in Normandy could be called the spiritual home of "B" Squadron then it was the fields near Cresserons, a small village about a mile and half east of Douvres la Deliverande. From here the Squadron would sally forth to battle and thence as faithfully return to refit, lick its wounds and drink the local "Calvados" in nearby Lion sur Mer.

You will recall that no sooner had "The Buffs" touched down in France than the regiment was dispatched piecemeal over the entire front. The initial bridgehead had been made. Now was to begin that inch by inch drive to enlarge it—that long, bitter slogging match, rarely equalled later in intensity or horror, and to which the subsequent break-out though far more spectacular was a "pushover" with the greater cost already dearly paid. Every day a bloody battle and "We must have flame-throwers". This was the universal cry. Within two days of landing then "B" Squadron had been attached to 8th Corps on the East side of the Bridgehead and on 26 June after only four days at St. Gabriel the Crocs clattered away to a field just South of Cresserons at 033795 preliminary to their first action on the next day.

The key to "B" Squadron's activities during the next few weeks was Caen. In Caen itself there were relatively few Germans but in all the host of villages, for a radius of some three miles around, the Germans had interposed between Caen and the British an extraordinarily strong system of strong points well manned by infantry, tanks and self-propelled guns. Moreover they were mutually supporting to an alarming degree. Division after division was to be flung in against these points before, in the end, they were liquidated at great cost of life. Before the great onslaught however there was some tidying up to be done—the odd place here and there essential to the take-off. What a deceptive phrase that term "tidying up". How often has it transpired to be more expensive than the great attacks.

7

DOUVRES **CHATEAU DE LANDEL**

KEY:-
ENEMY ARMS & TANKS.
BRITISH TANKS.
TANK MOVEMENT
GUN FIRE
SMALL ARMS
TREES

N

CPL. HUSHER

TP. SGT.

BREWED SHERMAN

LT. BROOK

CHATEAU

MORTARS & UNDER-GROUND SHELTERS

BANK

UNSUSPECTED TANKS

CAEN

Such a place was Chateau le Landel, some three miles north of Caen. Some three or four attacks were to be made in this tough nut before it cracked. One such unsuccessful attack had already been made when "B" Squadron came on the scene, and a fresh attack to take place on 27 June was laid on for one company of the East Yorkshires supported by one Troop of Crocodiles and two troops of tanks.

In another war there had been another Brooke. It was fitting perhaps that the first to lay down his life in "B" Squadron should be Lieut Raymond Brooke. 8 Troop had got the job.

A clear or accurate picture of what occured is difficult, built up as it is as much from deduction as from first hand information. It was an ill-fated party from the beginning. In those early days Crocodile tactics had still to be learned from the bitter experience of battle. The plan was hurried, and instead of close support on to the objective from the supporting tanks these were to give indirect support by acting on the flanks as anti-tank protection. It had been estimated that the position was held by one company of engineers whereas in fact it was an absolute nest of tanks (there were 14 in the chateau area itself), SPs, mortars and dug-in infantry positions besides numerous tanks on the flanks.

The 27 June was a blazing hot afternoon and in the F.U.P. area the moaning minnies were coming down pretty thick and pretty fast. If you were on foot like "Herby" or Roy Moss, trying to get a last minute ringside seat, and not yet attuned to judging their pitch as a matter of yards then it meant hitting the deck with a regularity anything but monotonous. Sydney Spearpoint was flitting around amongst them in a scout car.

For technical reasons the Crocs were unable to cross the Start Line on time and lost their infantry, who by the time the Crocs had started were held up about halfway to their objective.

Lieut Brooke on the left headed his Croc alongside a hedgerow and dashed straight to his objective, a long wall surrounding the Chateau. Unfortunately in the wall was a gate through which came a murderous anti-tank gun fire. Dug-in and unsuspected tanks just outside the

9

Chateau wall opened up. An incredible number of shots grazed his turret and hull but it was not until 20 yards off the objective that he bought it—a 75mm from a Mk IV inside the gate penetrated at almost point blank range and killed the gunner, Tpr Woodcock, outright. The crew baled out—Brooke was killed by machine gun fire as he climbed from the turret, but the rest somehow got back to our lines. Cpl Marsden had multiple shrapnel wounds. Tpr Dady having thus escaped had the extraordinarily bad luck later that same evening to be killed by a mortar whilst standing outside the RAP. Meanwhile Sgt Burton had rapidly become hors de combat from a jammed turret and a trailer wrapped around a tree, which had to be jettisoned. Only Corporal Hischier remained, putting up a creditable if inevitably an ineffectual show. He advanced as far as the line of trees, where our own infantry were pinned down by every kind of fire and could go no further. Moving over he shot up the wall on the left with 75mm in an effort to breach it for the infantry. Then on Sgt Burton's instructions he moved away out on the open right flank, alone and unsupported except for a Sherman which preceded him and rapidly brewed up. But as the infantry had now gone most definitely to ground for the day he pulled out, hotly pursued by AP shots. Crashing through a hedgerow a few yeards behind; the Start Line, and by now completely lost, he was stopped by Colonel Waddell with a cup of compo char. Out of the driver's seat climbed the likeable Freddy Roberts, "Cor aint arf hot there sir". And Cpl Vine, the gunner, most heartily concurred.

Well of course that wasn't too bright for a start. But then war never was very bright, especially in the beginning—experience makes you battle wise and the odds for your survival increase a shade, but to safely get the experience first of all you have to have the luck.

The next few days were spent in plans and preparations for a big attack. That is to say between the occasional egg and the odd steak. There was a little joint in Plumetot of which Peter Sander wotted where you could get delicious steaks—yeah even reputedly of beef et non pas de cheval. It wasn't allowed of course—but then what that is worth while ever is ? And couldn't Peter salve the conscience of the mess ?

On 28 June came the first of that long series of "on calls" which were to be the bane of the whole regiment right up to VE day. The Crocs were demanded and present in almost every operation fought, often without a definite task but "on call" if required. It is true that on some they were in fact not finally required and they neither flamed nor shot. Nevertheless it meant that they were incessantly within shell and mortar range and not a few of our casualties were sustained in these waiting parties. So that tension, whether physical or mental, could rarely be relaxed and then only for the briefest interval. It meant long hours spent in planning, dangerous recceing and movement—that is why every Croc officer to whom you talk is a virtual encyclopedia of campaign knowledge. For in that period of most intense fighting, the bridgehead, and for long afterwards there was only one regiment of flamethrowers on the continent, 141st R.A.C. (The Buffs), and every Corps clamouring for them hard. Moreover within those Corps every division was clamouring for them, every brigade and every battalion, and at this time getting them—so that virtually you ended up with one Croc to a platoon. One hour before zero this would solemnly be dismembered, giving unto each of two section commanders a set of tracks, to another the trailer and to the platoon commander the turret. What disasters this brought to infantry and Crocs will be elsewhere more apparent. Suffice it to say here that on a war establishment designed for a Squadron working as a whole, within a Regiment also working as a whole, on this establishment the problem of administration or of planning was a headache such as even Howard's Aspirin couldn't cure. You cannot split a jeep or a scout car and they are every bit as vital as a tank. When the Crocs did flame it was frontpage headlines—but this was only half the story, and they were frontline all the time.

Hence on the 28 June 6 and 7 Troops sallied out under Sydney to Cazelle in support of 3 British Div., 9 and 10 Troops toddling off under Nigel in support of 9 Canadian Brigade of 3 Canadian Division for an operation designed to drive through to Caen through Cambes and Buron. Once more however the mutually supporting strongpoints proved too formidable and the

11

operation shortly afterwards fell through. "B" Squadron once more rallying back to Cresserons (this time to a field just N.E. at 052801—a little nearer for the evening stroll to Lion sur Mer).

Here Rowland Beechey, already in "B" Squadron in England, rejoined the party to take over young Brooke's place and not so long after to suffer so very heroically the same fate. Superficially he was not "that B Squadron type" and yet for his sterling qualities he was most cordially embraced. Deeply religious he didn't smoke, drink, swear or philander. But his loyalty, his untiring energy, his courage and devotion to duty were of an order unexcelled. It is said that only the good die young—and there are many who when his name is mentioned now are one minute silent in their hearts.

CARPIQUET

Carpiquet could only have been pulled off unscathed by the superb and uncanny luck of the Playboys—any other Squadron would probably have bought the issue hook, line and sinker. Carpiquet cost the Canadian Infantry God knows what—but what went wrong with the German tanks and anti-tank guns on that day even God would be hard taxed to find an answer. All day long from "dawn to dewy eve" the Squadron pranced around, hunting the horrid Hun in flat open country without the slightest vestige of cover, ground which presented to the Germans probably their best field of fire in Normandy (the great airfield at Carpiquet) and ended up completely unsupported mixing it with fanatical SS guys crawling all over them. Yet at the end of the day only two casualties to personnel had been suffered and these not from enemy action. Lovely !

On the evening of 1 July then behold "B" Squadron minus 8 Troop throwing a careless *au revoir* to the paramours and fleshpots of Cresserons, pushing off for an uncomfortable night on the outskirts of Bretteville L' Orgueilleuse before having a crack at Carpiquet Aerodrome on the 3 July. Sgt Dallman had brought along the C.O's tank and a screach of brakes betokened the arrival of Herbert Waddell with his Bohemiam Tac HQ—a bedraggled jeep and the two fastest scouts cars in the 141. For there was nothing he liked more than to take a peek.

For operation "OTTAWA" the Squadron was theoretically divided in two in support of 7 Canadian Infantry Brigade, but in fact the two parties were to remain quite close to each other and in view. Spearthing with old Bonko to give support took the party on the right with 6 and 9 Troops. On the left Nigel had 7 and 10 Troops. There was no definite task in the initial phase, the idea being to motor along some way behind the infantry in case of accidents.

Long before dawn on 3 July Tpr Simmler was checking

13

up his guns, Fossey was testing his ignition, Cpl Waters revving up his engine and swearing like.... ...., Marfell was chatting over the air to Sgt Douse. Nippy Chips, doing L.O. to Brigade, was soon coming over loud and clear—could you ever mistake that clear perky voice over the air ? "Hullo Dog One Eight I got you first time, Out." Unfailing, never off net by one hairsbreadth.

There is a ridge running N.W. from St. Mauvieu, the perfect "School solution" for the hull-down. But the infantry wanted the Crocs closer. So in the bright. sunshine, naked as new born babes, over the top they came. Fanned out in the flat cornfields and landing ground this side of Carpiquet. Where the mortars blossomed orange and the black plumes of earth shot skywards from the shells. Where the Messerschmidt played vulture overhead. Fanned out and waited tensely—a rendezvous with death.

Nigel had already lost 10 Troop, which had turned off left and crossed the railway. The troop commander's tank was hopelessly bogged, Sgt Vernon was ditched too and could only extricate himself by jettisoning the trailer. Sgt Pipkin, muttering "Well f....... this for a lark" and all the unprintable rest, had slipped off on his own to join Nigel but he had not yet caught up. Peter Sander was the next to get his Croc ditched, He handed it over to Sgt Norrington, much to the latter's disgust, and switched tanks.

First assignment came to Sydney who farmed it out to Mike Henderson. The infantry were held up just short of a bunker the other side of the St Mauvieu—Caen Road. Mike bowled over with his troop, had a chat with the infantry captain some fifty yards away from the bunker. He decided that he could only get his own Croc on to it and went in giving the hot squirt for all he was worth. Whoever was in there didn't stand one earthly—ammunition went up inside and the whole thing was a blazing conflagration for hours. As he returned once more "to heel" another urgent call came over for flame on a hangar some 500 yards to the S.W. of this bunker and Sydney slipped the leash on Peter.

Now Pete in action would distract you from the Can-Can of the Folies Bergeres. He had only one technique. very spectacular and extremely effective. It was simply

14

to go bull-headed for the object of his disaffection giving everything he had the whole way, 75mm, Besa, flame, his own revolver and a vocabulary as voluble as it was extensive. So it was now. The rest of the Squadron forgot the battle and turned in their cupolas to watch this fire—raising display by Peter and Sgt Decent—Sgt Decent of course was not to be outdone in ferocity ,not even by Peter. Not satisfied with brewing it up from the front they brewed it up on both sides—by the fortune of heaven they did not go round the back where, all unknown then, there lurked a dirty 88. Then came dashing back with the sort of tone, "Well come on I've done that— now what do you want me to do next ?" Dear old Peter.

Meanwhile Sgt. Norrington, left if you remember holding the Troop Commander's baby, was in a pickle and thinking no doubt just what he would do to a pint next time he set eyes on his brewer's dray. First thing he did no doubt was to put the kettle on for a cup of char— you never saw a man drink tea like Sgt Norrington. Then he rang up Sydney on the set and said sort of, look here what about a spot of recovery, can't stay here all day you know or I shall miss the party, now what about the old ARV coming up here and pulling us out ? "What's your map reference ?" from Sydney. "Dunno sir," "Well why the............not ?" "Sorry sir. Sunray took the maps". "Well never do it again". "No sir". "Well you'll have to wait, that's all there is to it". Well I mean to say—Sgt Norrington wait when the other chaps were in !

There was all the filth imaginable coming down around that spot but old "Hardy" spotted Captain Moss's tank a good 300 yards away and decided on a scrounge with just the personal touch. Ever seen Hardy run— it's a sight worth watching. But it didn't look too good that day, the only upright human figure in sight and the bursts all round him. But he made it alright. "Come over and give us a tow sir ? Go on sir—won't take a minute". You never could resist Sgt Norrington and old Bonko went. This was the first. How many more times in action were the HQ tanks to tow out the recalcitrant Crocs and recover them under fire—tow them out until the engines lost their guts, tow them till the shackles

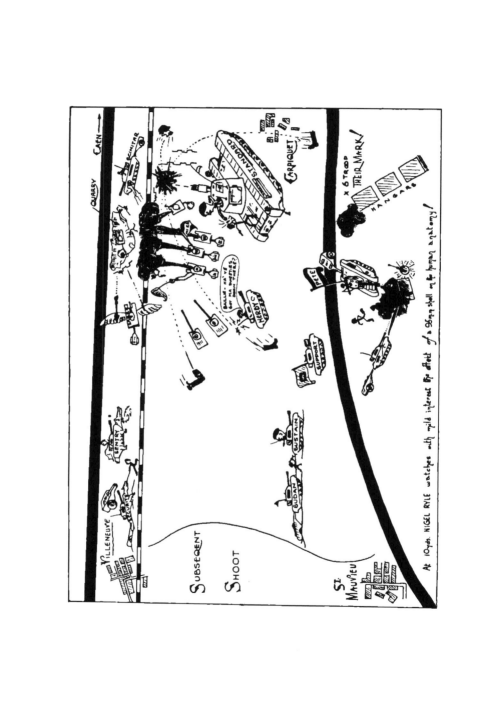

wouldn't take the pins, but always get them mobile, get them rolling. Because of it's trailer a Croc will get ditched or bogged long before any other tank—but Jesus, sometimes the people who didn't know them expected them to turn somersaults.

Now Nigel stepped into the ring. A nearby Sherman suddenly spied a nest of Germans in a quarry by the Caen-Bayeux road, which said monstrosities showed unmistakeable signs of vicious life now that our infantry on the tail of the barrage had swept on. The Sherman asked Nigel to fix'em—he said "You bet." There were no infantry so Beck with 7 Troop just went in without. He poked his own nose in the quarry and gave them hell, burning some and flushing more as target practice for the other tanks. Then came his undoing—he went right in the quarry and couldn't get out, couldn't move left or right, could not reverse through the narrow entry with his trailer. Well, there he was in a pretty hot strong-point with no infantry to clear it and unable to do a thing. To get out he had to jettison his trailer, but there wasn't room—so the novel expedient was tried of shooting away the link by Sgt Brandi's gunner. But Crocs are tricky things and they didn't shut off the Hopkinson Valve. The first shot made a hole straight through the neck and in a split second the whole issue was covered in blazing fuel, pressure fed. The heat was so intense that there was no alternative but to bale out, Germans or no Germans. The co-driver Hards looked out through the pannier door, saw the flames, decided it was impossible to get out that way and hopped it straight through the hatch. Simpson the driver looked out through the hatch, saw the flames, decided it was impossible to get out that way and hopped it straight through the pannier door. In the turret Davenport with his usual sangfroid waited till everyone was out, picked up his pipes, coolly traversed the turret to reach the driving compartment and through the pannier door made an "exit" which would have done credit even to A.R.G.S. Westwell. Sgt Brandi dashed in to collect the crew whilst Sgt Maddock gave them covering fire. Lieut Beck and his gunner Christieson were badly burned.

Then came the scene that stole the whole show. Nigel was sort of looking on at this party and letting off

17

the odd round. He glanced casually down from his cupola over the side and saw a German some ten yards away drawing a bead with his rifle, just on his first pressure in fact to take a pot right at Nigel's head. Well Nigel wasn't the sort of chap who stood for any disrespect or nonsense to an officer—besides his moustache might have been singed. He popped down momentarily in the turret and went off the deep end. That guy needed a pretty hefty lesson. Round swung the turret and—oh! Nigel how could you—in split seconds a whole 95mm shell was heading dead centre for the Boche. And Nigel watching with mild interest its effect on the human anatomy at such short range. No excuses Nige—we heard it all on the "A". "Give the bastard the f——95". The next minute all hell was let loose around his tank. Nigel suddenly discovered that he was sitting right in the middle of a well camouflaged company position left almost untouched by the advance. Literally dozens of Germans sprung out of concealment in the long grass. They stalked his tank, climbed on his tank, did everything except knock it out. Bloodthirsty Mulvaney, his gunner, followed up his 95mm with a Besa burst of 50 which began on a Hun's backside and crept up—the body was found later in two clean halves. The Shermans joined in and shot them down. Waddell joined in and shot them down. As usual he gave you a good treat of fire orders on the A set before passing them on the I.C. "**Shoot** the ruddy bastards down Sgt Dallman, shoot the bastards down". Nigel performed feats of agility. With one hand he was dealing with Germans on the engine deck, with the other holding the microphone and yelling to Sydney for assistance, forgot to switch over and exhorted Mulvaney on the "A" set to "Give the buggars hell". About twenty-five were accounted for by Besa fire alone. Spearthing sent Mike over at the gallop and 6 Troop dashed straight in shooting flame left, right and centre. Sgt Pipkin, persistent ever, came up at this moment, triumphant in his search at last. He required no order/ but just let everything go. Very soon the party was well under control—later were found charred discarded equipment, burned bodies, bodies killed by Besa and HE, and one that had just died of fright. Nigel asked for infantry

18

to come and really mop up the area but owing to casualties most unfortunateley none were available, and the position remained for a long time in German hands as a nuisance pocket to the Canadians after Carpiquet itself was captured. Non-availability of infantry must inevitably lead to lack of positive dividends from flame.

By now the flame was just about running out, anyway the operation had pretty well come to a standstill. The Crocs were released to a position once more just behind the ridge. On the way back Mike ditched his Croc and spent a hectic half hour getting it out with the rest of his troop. At one point a Messerschmidt swooped down on them—it's an amazing thing but you can get twelve men under the same trailer. Ask Mike.

The day's work was not yet quite complete. Over on the right one Canadian Battalion was having a sticky time in one particular spot, and it was decided to give them an indirect shoot from the northern part of the ridge.

Rapid calculations with protractors and landmarks for range and direction. Then all opened up together. Out of the setting sun Mike was bowling a good length ball and keeping it up—some of the best air bursts ever seen. And on this note Carpiquet ended for the Crocs.

OFF NET

Mechanically badly battered the Squadron harboured the night at Norrey en Bassin and on the next day, 4 July, returned to Cresserons. But there is no peace for the wicked. Straightway the Squadron had to get down to planning and refitting for Operation "Charnwood", designed to begin almost immediately afterwards. "Charnwood" was a highly complicated attack on a three division front with colossal artillery support to take CAEN. The Squadron could only muster four troops and in spite of all protests these were parcelled out over the whole front with no definite task but to be in reserve if required. 6 Troop under command of Roy Moss were under 3 British Division on the left whose immediate objective was the shattered woods and village of Lebisey. Nippy Chips took 8 Troop, once more complete under Beechey, in support of 176 Brigade, and Major Spearpoint 9 Troop in support of 197 Brigade. These Brigades belonged to the ill-fated 59 Division which was going down the centre through Cambes and Epron. Captain Ryle was over on the right with 10 Troop in support of 7 Canadian Brigade coming down through Gruchy and Buron. The Squadron thus found itself in the impossible situation of being split up over four brigades on three divisional fronts. The tactical and administrative disadvantage of such piecemeal allocation were to be sadly proved next day.

On the 6th Roy Moss moved down with his party to just north of Lebisey and on the next day the remainder of the Squadron moved out to their various assignments. Sydney Spearpoint and John Dean moved to Anisy, Nigel moving to an F.U.P. between Villons les Buisson and Vieux Cairon. In the early morning John Dean pushed forward with 8 Troop and lined up alongside the orchard at the back edge of Cambes. Sydney pushed over to just east of Villons le Buisson.

In the early morning too the thunder of the heavies. The drumfire of the massed 25 pounders—that ceaseless

20

roll of theirs, urgent, pressing. The crack of the mortar teams, the chatter-chatter of the machine guns. The angry bang of the Shermans and the lovely brew-up when they hit their mark. The battle was on and the bell was already tolling. Back came the answer. The great black spumes and the roaring crash from the 150 millies, the minnies wailing in batch after batch and crash, the red flashes from the German tanks and SPs that swarmed near La Bijude all out to get the Sherman tanks.

Jerry had Cambes absolutely taped and gave it everything he had. The South Staffs forming up took a colossal packet. There is a graveyard there now. And later, as they buried those long, long rows of dead, one of their comrades said "This isn't war sir—its just sheer mass murder".

John sat tight there, waiting. There is nothing worse than waiting—hour after hour, all day and sometimes half the night. Now and then he'd send a little perky back-chat on the air. After a somewhat interrupted breakfast of undercooked compo sausages in the lee of his scout car Colonel Waddell came over from Sydney's area for a chat. A few minutes later John was summoned on the air and his tank disappeared around the corner up the railway track as far as the Halt, for a confab with the Shermans which were hulldown there.

The infantry had got no further than the forward edge of Cambes. After enormous casualties from mortaring and shelling they ran straight into heavy fire from an extensive trench system of some 200 yards, strongly and fanatically held across the open fields just west of La Bijude and south of Cambes, not so very far away from where John was now standing scratching his head. It was now seriously suggested that the position be flamed by 8 Troop alone supported by a mere sixteen infantry men already well and truly pinned. John's wiser counsels fortunately prevailed. He pointed out that the position demanded a full scale attack by at least a battalion of infantry with artillery support, and that to put the Crocs in without adequate infantry to kill the enemy and occupy the ground was merely to lose the Crocs on the strong anti-tank gun defences to no purpose whatsoever. A sound axiom rarely disputed later after bitter experience—"No infantry,

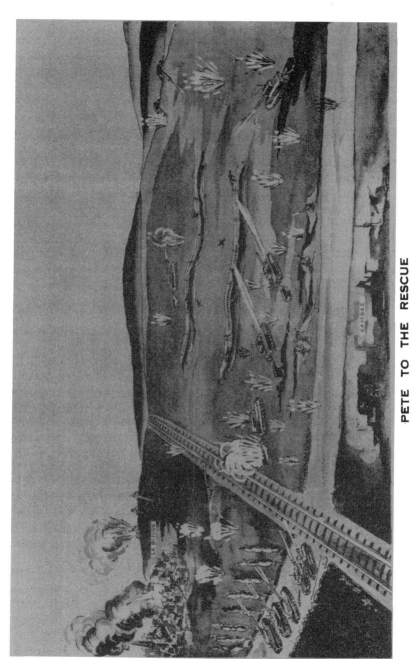

PETE TO THE RESCUE

no show". However it was typical of John that he should seek confirmation of such a view. He rang up Colonel Waddell, still just around the corner, who strolled up himself and gave his most unqualified support.

That to some was the last impression of John. Leaning forward against the back of a Sherman in the sunshine, tin helmet tilted back, a slightly worried face looking at his own patent map board, tugging at his patent chinagraph device—oblivious to all the stuff falling round about him.

By late evening a plan was finally knocked out with a new battalion, the South Lancs, and the 13/18 Hussars. Meanwhile Sydney had brought 9 Troop to the same orchard and was trying desperately to get released from 197 Brigade in order to augment John's pitifully small force.

This very gallant action fell into two phases. At about 1930 hours Lieut Beechey led 8 Troop alongside the railway and crashed over the start line just east of it at 023737, supported by fire from John Dean and the 13/18 Hussars from the road. Rowland Beechey had started on his absolute classic of coolnesss, courage, tank control and troop control. After some fifty yards he realised that the infantry had not set out with him so coolly took his troop back, collected them and set off again. Almost immediaately Cpl Hischier lost a bogey assembly from a German "bazooka" and was then penetrated by a 75mm straight through the flame-gun ball mounting which killed outright both driver and co-driver, L/C Roberts and Tpr Pitt. The tank "brewed up" and the turret crew baled out—Cpl Hischier, Cpl Vine and Tpr Halley. They lay doggo for a time then, very badly burned, managed to crawl to a RAP. Right from the start Beechey was getting unignited shots from his flame-gun but he carried on, getting his Sgt to ignite them. He saw the plight of his Corporal and put out smoke to shield the crew as they baled out. A 75mm went smack into his gearbox, completely dislocating the steering and setting the tank on fire. Cool as ice Roland Beechey pulled the CO2 bottle, evacuated his crew under mortar and small arms fire, watched the flames go out, climbed back in and still carried on. The steering had gone, and the tank was stuck in second gear. Nevertheless, moving in wide

23

circles, he continued to give 75 and Besa support whilst directing his Sgt until the latter's flame gave out.

Then into this twilight arena Sydney and Peter roared and clattered to the rescue. Released from 197 Brigade only minutes before and without any knowlege of the plan or ground they came belting up and over the the railway, charging in with a furious onslaught of steel and flame. The flaming was magnificent. Peter just "went to town". Never before or since did such a "rod" of flame spew forth from any Croc as that which Staples now sent seething and roaring over cowering Germans in their trenches. Serve you right you bastards! Into the trenches, over the trenches, into dugouts and round corners the stuff boiled and licked—old Staples was down there in his seat muttering Cockney imprecations as he sweated with the gun, heaving it this way and that against the heavy stiffness of the pipes. And into this blazing wrath Partridge the gunner was slamming out the 75s as fast as he could go. Sgt Norrington was doubling up, making up for what he'd missed at Carpiquet. Sgt. Decent's pressure gone—these were the early days when Crocs were just about as constant as fickle womankind— but making up for it with Besa and HE liberally applied. Rowland Beechey, halted now, was using up his last few rounds. And now in this weird setting of dusk and burning flame the infantry came on, went in, passed through, surged on.

John went over and towed Beechey out, the rest of the party rallying back. Then with Sgt Rowe, who volunteered, he set out on foot to get the form on recovering Cpl Hischier's trailer. Complete darkness had fallen now but the light from three burning tanks made them have to crawl. Hearing the cry of a wounded man Captain Dean crawled over in that direction, touched off an "S" mine and died shortly after. For the first and last time Nippy Chips was "off net."

Before he died Sgt Rowe attempted to lift him up and carry him but this was no good. So Sgt Rowe went back and brought up his tank to a position nearby. As the crew dismounted however the silhouetted tank brought down such a hail of mortars that Sgt Rowe decided to take it back and try

24

again on foot. Now was to come a tragic repetition. Rowland Beechey, hearing what had happened, himself took charge of the party which set off again. Again a wounded man cried out, Beechey crawled towards him and he too set off an "S" mine, receiving severe leg injuries. God knows how many chaps that minefield accounted for. There was no RAP nearby but he himself, carried on a tank, directed the crew with great fortitude to a RAP some miles back. He died next day, a brave and gallant officer.

A sad day for "B" Squadron. Both John Dean and Beechey were mentioned in dispatches. A few days later Nigel was censoring mail and came across a letter written to a vicar in Ashford by L/C Harris, the operator in Beechey's tank. An extract, given here, is the most fitting final comment. "On the 7 July 1944 Lieut Beechey briefed 8 Troop for what he described as a most outstanding operation. We were to clear a heavily fortified area on the approaches to Caen, then the Armoured Divisions would take Caen itself. To us Caen was an "ogre" and almost a legend, as it was the pivot of the first German defence line in Western France.

At 0400 hours on July 8th we moved up to the front, and by 0500 hrs. we were in position, waiting to be used if the necessity arose. It was our first taste of action, and on Lieut Beechey's tank it was the first action for all of us. We had hardly any sleep for that night previous and as the afternoon dragged on Lieut Beechey cheered us up as best he could, and also took turns on "wireless watch" although he need not have done so. This gave the gunner and myself a chance to get a little sleep.

At 1900 hours Lieut Beechey went on recce and at 1925 hours he returned, jumped into his tank and gave the order to advance. There was no time for briefing, all we knew were the few details of the defence layout and that a Squadron of the 13/18 Hussars was 'shooting us in'. We advanced about 50 yards over the Start Line and then realised the infantry wern't following us in, we returned, consolidated, and went in again, this time followed by the South Lancs. We must have had every anti-tank gun ranged on us, as after withdrawing the first time we had given our position away. We had hardly started firing when a flail tank went up in flames on our right, and the troop corporal's tank on our left also got it. Lieut Beechey ordered me to lay 2 in. smoke round the brewed up tank so the crew could get away. Then whilst loading HE 75 I suddenly found a round loaded itself! Then the driver reported no oil pressure and smoke began pouring out of the back. We knew we'd been hit and after seeing that the enemy was on our left, Lieut Beechey, after releasing the CO_2 bottle gave orders to bale out on the right. I grabbed the rum ration (No. 1. priority), the slidex and we baled out. We were getting mortared and sniped at. Luckily the CO_2 bottles extinguished the fire and we got back into the tank. Lieut Beechey then ordered us to advance, we had no left steering and the tank was jammed in second gear, but we made a wide sweep round. The flame gun wasn't working properly so the co-driver got out under fire and increased the hand control. We fired the 75 and Besa, but the flame-gun was out of action. Eventually we turned a complete circle and got to a high embankment and couldn't go any further. Then Lieut Beechey ordered the turret to be traversed and we engaged any likely targets until the turret itself jammed.

At about 2130 hours an HQ troop tank came and took us off. As soon as we got to the base Lieut Beechey held a thanksgiving service. During this time Captain Dean had gone to look at the trailer of the corporal's tank. Suddenly one of the HQ Sgts came back and said that Captain Dean had been blown up on a mine. At that moment we saw someone in the bushes and the co-driver and I went to investigate, we found one of our own infantrymen who was wounded and we brought him in and made him comfortable. During our absence Lieut Beechey took a few men and went out in search of Captain Dean. About half hour later the party brought Lieut Beechey back on a stretcher, and he had also struck the same minefield as Captain Dean. We all piled on HQ tank and as there wasn't room for us inside the gunner and I lay on the track covers, shielding Lieut Beechey who was lying aross the driving hatches. Then the mortars and small arms fire opened up and we had to get away quickly. We had no morphia syringe, so we gave Lieut Beechey the tablets instead. We were lost and didn't know our way back, but kept on what we thought to be the right path. During this time Lieut Beechey was in terrible pain but he refused to lose consciousness and directed us back to base. If it weren't for his courage and leadership, I doubt if we'd ever have got back."

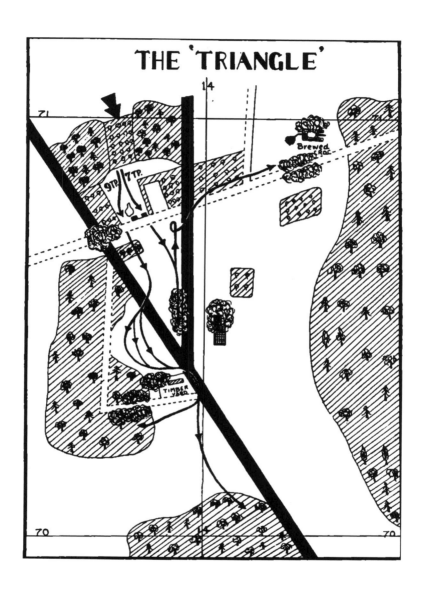

THE 'TRIANGLE'

THE TRIANGLE

After Cambes the whole Squadron returned to Cress-erons where they remained from the 9th of July to the 16th. It was a period however not without incident, for the cast was now augmented by the appearence of those two notable actors in the play, none other than Lieut Harry Barrow ("The first time I met her—") and Lieut Tony Ward. The former took over 7 Troop and the "young man" was destined later to re-form 8 Troop. Harry was "not one of these posh blokes"—but he did reckon to know something about cricket. A Hampshire product with a big ruddy complexioned face and an outside in noses that went with it, married, with a sizeable shoe business. His fund of stories just went on for ever and every single one merited the proverbial halfcrown. An invaluable asset for the long series of stag parties imposed during a campaign. Moderately in his cups in a good mood he would pan Michael, in a bad mood he was all for going out to pan a few "back liners". A good scout. Tony, the mighty atom, was a different type. Of York-shire breed he showed the peculiarities of that bulldog strain. A little devil mind you but serious, earnest, grimly determined. It was a cinch to "take the mike" out of him—he rose to the bait at any time and then just as ser-iously and laboriously would scheme to do the same. Still with a little training he took a passing fancy to the bottle and in the end **talked** far more of the fairer sex even than the others. Even so "Ah doan't intend to lie with any woman till ah'm wed".

Here too Captain Shearman joined the Squadron for a while.

'B' Squadron were now to go further afield and cross the famous "Pegasus Bridge" in support of the 5 Seaforths of the 51st Highland Div., their object being to capture the triangle SE of Escoville formed by cross-roads 136706, 140706, and 140702, preliminary to Troarn. Thus on the night of the 15/16 July once more without an 8 Troop the Squadron moved out from Cresserons, heading east of the Canal de Caen and the river Orne. There was appalling darkness, fog, dust and traffic congestion, and for a long time it looked as if they would never reach their destination before daylight, vital for security and surprise. But in some uncanny way Roy Moss as Recce Officer somehow kept them crawling and finally brought them into an orchard at 133724, about a mile north and slightly west of the Start Line, and some 200 yards from enemy positions in the east. That is all except his own tank which fell out on the way and was left in charge of Sgt Jake Morley. Here they lay up for the day.

This was to be the first case of a complete Croc Squadron effort and as such was to prove a great success. In spite of its darker side it was also to be the funniest thing on record. The whole event was so crowded with numerous smaller events all happening at the same time that the chronicling of it must inevitably fall short. The plan was based on the large element of surprise which would transpire from the sudden advent of Crocs in most unlikely tank country, and on the knowledge that the German listening posts regularly went off for their breakfast at 0800 hrs.

The original plan was as follows. Roy Moss was to lead the Crocs through a maze of woods, hedges and orchards up to the orchard at 136709 where it formed a sort of gap between two woods. The orchard was an area of No Man's Land, the balance of power heavily weighted on the German side. From here the troops would fan out left and right. On the right 6 Troop closely supported by fire from 9 Troop were to get a company on to the cross-roads at 136706 and some 200 yards forward. On the left 7 Troop closely supported by 10 Troop were to get a company on to the cross-roads at 140708. They were then to come down their respective roads and get "B" and "D" companies on to the apex. In actual fact 6 Troop developed trailer trouble at the last minute and changed roles with 9 Troop. Of the left more later.

On the 15th Sydney Spearpoint and Roy Moss did a recce of our own F.D.L.S. The "yeoman" colonel was most concerned to impress on them the need to step carefully as the ground was covered in trip wires designed to set off warning flares. "Now you must step carefully see, use a stick and feel for them gently, or you'll set em off and bring all the ......in creation down. Like this, see. Teach you to be infantrymen yet, what !" At this third tentative prod of demonstration up zoomed reds, greens, whites and all the colours of the rainbow—and down came all the ......in creation. From here Roy set out to recce the route to the Start Line. Now old Bonko did many creditable things in his time but this rates high among them. An infantry patrol took him as far as the northern edge of the orchard where they halted, "From now on sir it's all yours". Now if you've got a backside like a junior barrage balloon and your Boy Scout days are long since over you don't enthusiastically go playing cowboys and Indians in broad daylight with Germans just licking their lips at the sight of a nice bit of juicy target flesh. But Bonko just rustled along into their lines, saw what he wanted to see, and rustled back to where the waiting patrol received him back with somewhat mild surprise.

At 0700 hrs. the Squadron began moving up to the Start Line. At 0805 hrs. with guns blazing they emerged from the orchard, advancing steadily with the infantry. Within three minutes P.W. were coming in. On the right the advance went according to plan and the Sander type. Sgt Norrington stood back at the pond giving covering fire to Peter and Sgt Decent who went in with customary élan to flame the German positions at the cross-roads, catching them in the midst of breakfast preparations. They killed many and ousted others. Pausing only to shoot up a section of Germans moving behind a hedgerow across their front they carried on in the direction of the apex. Sgt Decent and Peter crossed the road, Sgt Decent skirting the wood and flaming as he went to clear the snipers, Peter covering him from the middle of the clearing and Sgt Norrington firing for all he was worth down the centre of the road. Close behind them 6 Troop pumping out Besa and 75 in all directions. The troop then re-formed and went in to make an absolute bonfire of the timber yard, thus establishing the infantry firmly on the final objective and giving Peter a chance to look for souvenirs whilst Sgt Decent machine gunned further for snipers in the wood.

31

On the left Harry in the difficult country went too far forward and missed the cross roads. He carried on however flaming and gunning with great ferocity to the road, knocking out a 75mm anti-tank gun in the first few seconds, and then swept up the inside of the triangle to the apex where he too established the infantry and continued to give them magnificent Besa support. Meanwhile Nigel travelling close behind, was quick to realise what had happened and diverted 10 Troop to the left hand cross-roads. Lieut Mason ditched his tank so Pipkin carried on with Sgt Vernon in support. What happened to him then is a matter of conjecture. With strict orders not to cross the road "Pip" nevertheless was inveigled into dashing off to flame some distant woods. His tank hit two Tellers and was then brewed up by bazooka fire. On the next day German stretcher bearers brought in the bodies of Sgt Pipkin and L/C/ Murray but of the other three— Watts, Deverson and Jones—not a trace was ever found. Not until a fortnight later was it possible to get near the tank. Sgt Vernon had just got across the cross-roads when he took a large-size bazooka through the turret, wounding the gunner and the operator, Smith and Butterworth. Sgt. Vernon gave the order to bale out but was killed outright by a mortar bomb as he himself was getting out. The driver, Bishop, took the tank back across the cross-roads, got the wounded off to a RAP and later drove the tank back to harbour.

Unable to get either Pipkin or Vernon on the air Nigel sent 7 Troop to the cross-roads where they found the infantry already installed in the little orchard just the other side. Harry picked up a wounded infantryman and set off to take him along the lateral road. At that moment however from the other side of the cross roads a strong body of Germans opened up and another Croc attack was put in to clear the road running north east. Whilst 7 Troop went up the road flaming everything Nigel shot up the woods and did a pincer round the back, so that the position was cleared out. Nigel then became a little careless and strolled on unconcerned with Roy in search of Mausers. With startling suddenness two hefty Germans sprang out from the undergrowth in front of them and— surrendered.

Meanwhile just as any thunderbolt Jake Morley broke in upon the stage. Left, if you remember, on the way he had at last repaired his tank and now pounded along to rejoin the herd. At the harbour of the day before he caught up with their spoor, chased along the trackmarks till they brought him to the triangle. Here Jake saw that some sort of a scrap was going on and that was good enough for him. With a tallyho he jumped straight in. Now littered around the triangle were some derelict German tanks from earlier fighting. Jake pasted these tanks to hell and back, stopping every now and then to triumphantly announce "Just knocked out a f   great big Tiger on the left" or remarks to that effect. But completely deaf to any message sent to him.

Meanwhile Peter too had been busy once again. The company commander asked him to give protection to him at the apex whilst his men dug in. So Peter sat in the apex whilst Sgt Decent went up the road some two hundred yards. Peter would occasionally say to Sydney on the air, "Look here I can't see any more Germans here. Oh yes I can—there's one just crawling across the road. Just wait a sec." Then trouble developed down the little side road leading past the timber yard. So Sgt Norrington and Peter went up there and flamed them out. Only one more casualty was sustained, Tpr Williams of Captain Shearman's tank, who was killed outright by mortar fire as he dismounted from his tank.

The whole operation had been a great success, many Germans being killed or captured, and it won for the Squadron the personal thanks and congratulations of GOC 1st Corps, General Crocker.

In the late afternoon the Squadron returned to the orchard at 134724, a most unhealthy spot from every point of view. Though not subsequently required ten days were spent there under almost incessant mortar, artillery and indirect machine gun fire. Units in the same field and adjacent fields were taking considerable casualties but for a long time the luck of the Squadron held, only Tpr Gregg catching a bullet in the leg. What really did cause havoc were the dive-bombing activities of hordes of mosquitoes, from which there was no respite. Rub yourself in filthy smelling ointment from the Doc, pull blankets round your head, try to sleep inside the tank—still they came on for their pound of flesh, weaving, buzzing and shrieking in your ear. Covered in purple ointment and a myriad bumps Sydney's face was unrecognisable. Sleep was impossible. Nerves were getting frayed. Then on the night of 26 July came their big brothers—the German bombers.

It was pitch dark as they came in, flying pretty low and dropping flares till the whole area was light as day. They cruised around dropping hefty containers of deadly anti-personnel bombs all round, going for the guns. Ammunition dumps were soon going up, adding colour to the scene. It looked as if they were going to miss this tiny little field, till a lone Bren gun tracer flickered up into the sky. Whoosh! In came the second wave with deadly accuracy. L/C Revell, considerate conscientious "father" of 6 Troop, on guard with Vincent, Pearson and Hudson stood beside his tank, heard the approaching whistle and told them to dive beneath. Next second he was picked up bodily by blast and flung headlong underneath himself. Sgt Wetherell had slung a bivouac sheet hammockwise beneath the tank and there wasn't all that much room. "This is it" said Vincent as another one came down but it hit the glacis plate, which saved their lives. Sgt Wetherell's bivouac sheet and blankets were honeycombed with holes and there was shrapnel everywhere but nobody was hurt. They simply rained down. Within minutes upwards of 60 bombs fell in this small area of some hundred by a hundred yards. They fell on the tracks, on the trailers, behind the tanks, in front of the tanks. Peter Sander had just decided that sight-seeing was perhaps not quite on when he too took a kick in the pants which knocked him underneath his tank, Sgt Decent too. A whole container dropped right beside their troop. By now most of the echelon were staying here as well. One dropped straight through the jeep. Tpr Cross was sleeping in his scout car when one hit the side panel and caved it in—in so far as he did not remain sleeping the story is somewhat spoiled. Lieut Tony Ward and Douglas Peacock were in a hole beside the other scout car when one dropped right alongside and smashed up all the sump. Not one man but didn't have some fantastic near escape.

In all this Sgt Norrington heard a shout from Major Spearpoint's tank and went over to find the Major badly hit, Sgt Douse even worse. Sgt Rowe took a splinter in the thigh. Into the more tender portions of Rispin and Mulvaney little pieces of red hot metal buzzed and bit. Mike underneath his tank took some in the shoulder and turned over to find his gunner with a fractured skull and other wounds. He started to bandage him up. Within a short time everything was organised. Davenport was strolling round checking up. Cpl Mulvaney rushed around for the half-track, on which the "young man" came up and the casualties were got away. Those two excellent sergeants Rowe and Douse did not return. Months later Sydney came back over but as Squadron Leader in the 7th RTR, where he served with distinction and renewed his bibulous acquaintanceship with 141. Michael was to come back later to 'B' Squadron. When day broke all the trucks were found to have flat tyres, pools of FTF were leaking from the punctured drums, and pools of water from the radiators. Whittingham was cursing blue murder about his precious water truck. But by and large the price had been astonishingly light.

On the next day Captain Ryle became Major Ryle and commanded the Squadron with gallantry and distinction to the end. Securing their release he took the party back to Cresserons that day.

COUNTRY GALLOPS !

This was to be the last sojourn at Cresserons and lasted until the 7th of August. At Escoville Lt. Douglas Peacock had rejoined the Squadron from England where he had been detained with injuries to his hand. A quiet, handsome, clever, hardworking, cheerful guy ("You comical sod" Kirkpatrick christened him) he too was of the finest English type. He stayed for only a few days, going to RHQ as BTA, but he will reappear. At Cresserons Capt. George Storrar came over from 'A' Squadron to act as 2i/c. Most of George's activities have no doubt been chronicled elsewhere—that great big young Scottish farmer whose "tanking" knowledge and ability bowed to none. Tony Ward meanwhile re-formed 8 Troop with Sgt Morley and Cpl Durno as his aides, Lt. Philpott took over 6 Troop. Sgt Norrington took up permanent residence as troop sergeant of HQ and Sgt "Jack" Huxtable took his place in 9 Troop. Jackie Bateman now became the monarch of the air. Square three !

On 6 August 'B' Squadron came under command of 2 Canadian Corps for "Totalise" and was allotted under command of 33 Tank Brigade to 51 Highland Division, moving to Cormelles, a suburb of Caen, on the 7th of August. "Totalise", in which the 144 RAC were to distinguish themselves so well, was a daring night attack astride the Caen—Falaise road, with the armour leading in two columns either side of the road and infantry in Priests behind. The object on the left was to secure a firm base from which to launch the Polish Armoured Division. Thus during the night 7/8 August 51 Division were to secure Longuichon Wood, Garcelles, Cramesnil and St Aignan-de-Cramesnil, the whole area to be mopped up on the moring of the 8 August and made firm in the East by the capture of Secqueville La Campagne. It was in this mopping up phase that the Squadron was to be used, originally with 5th Seaforths with whom they had achieved such success west of Troarn.

From Cormelles that night they watched the superb night-bombing of the RAF, the Bofor tracers that soared gracefully through Monty's moonlight down the axis of advance and the great flashes of artillery at the sending and receiving ends. At 1000 hrs on the 8th the Crocs moved out to a position of readiness just west of the rubble that had been Le Bras, where the little shell-scarred calvary still stands. That fine general, Major General Rennie of the Highland Divison, eating a solitary breakfast in the ruins of a courtyard was suddenly besieged by Buffs.

From here looking back that morning they saw a great force of Forts come round the flank of Caen—then, no it couldn't be possible, wheel slowly round and drop the most colossal load of bombs on Cormelles itself. The echelon of course was still back there. They dropped them on the line of guns at the bottom of the echelon's field, causing absolute havoc. Tpr Humphrey, left out of battle as the survivor from Lt. Brooke's tank, was killed. Tprs Hartfield and McDougall were wounded. But the echelon jumped to it—you can't shake old steadies like Collins, or Ireson or Spicer very long. One fuel truck was burning fiercely and the heated bottles were being shot out just like torpedoes. Regardless of everything Sgt Little, who later got the MM, and L/C Knight first backed away the petrol truck packed close behind, then drove off the truck in front. Another fuel truck was burning at the hood—Sgt Little drove it off while L/C Knight got up behind and fought the fire out. It's not nice to play around with fire when you've got a load of FTF on board. The grass was all alight so they drove the whole echelon into another field and got cracking on the flat tyres. And that evening Speedy's echelon was at the appointed spot to meet the Crocs and fill them up.

The night attack had gone well and the infantry were on their forward objectives but Tilly La Campagne was still causing trouble in the rear and 5th Seaforths were called in to deal with this. It was finally decided to do the attack on Secqueville la Campagne with the Gordon Highlanders but the plan itself remained basically unchanged. This was for the two forward companies with one Squadron of Shermans from 148 RAC to go right through the village, leaving "D" Company with the Crocodiles to mop up the forward patches of the wood just west of the village. Flank protection was to be given by two Squadrons of 148 RAC, one on either side of the road leading into the village. A very thorough artillery programme was laid on to deal with the surrounding areas, La Hogue in particular. The plan was ready-made but the change-over was very hurried and naturally a bit confused. Nigel was kept champing at the bit so long at a procrastinated infantry 'O' Group that he was not able to to hold one himself with the Troop Commanders until 1610 hrs. With H hour at 1630 hrs. the Troops were not able to mate up properly with their opposite numbers and this added to the confusion.

Yet another element added to the general melee. The Poles, chafing at the leash, had been released over the Start Line a little earlier than originally planned and off they went in every direction gleefully rubbing their hands in anticipation—it was their first time in action over here. So that the whole attack was to be a glorious pandemonium of Polish tanks, 148 RAC tanks, Crocodiles and infantry all over the place.

If the plan did not go according to plan nevertheless it went quite effectively. Lickety-split cross-country the Squadron arrived in Garcelles Secqueville, swung right by the church, the tracks grinding horribly through the debris and threatening every minute to come off, into the fields and formed up behind the ridge just south east of Garcelles Secqueville. Colonel Waddell had joined in the party to have a little crack as well, and just as one driver experienced very obvious difficulty in turning off, over the air in unmistakeable Scottish tones to his own driver there came, "Now Ham that fellow's made a ballsup of it— now you just show them what a good driver *you* are".

As usual the Germans were where the defence overprint was blank, and as the Crocs topped the ridge in their advance the first 95mm brought out a dozen of them just ahead. Not finding 'C' Company 7 and 8 Troops found themselves supporting the forward companies instead. The attack went too far right and the "young man" was soon busy flaming just outside the village itself, getting results here equally well. Harry Barrow took on

Tony's original job, flaming and laying about him with very good effect. Nigel sent 10 Troop under George Storrar's paternal hand over the road to the left to flame up 7 Troop's original task. So that in spite of all the confusion both jobs were accomplished and an extra one as well. Whether they were necessary is another matter— the Germans were so "bomb-happy" and shot to hell that they were just streaming in anyhow. The Squadron then joined in with the Shermans to shoot up the isolated wood at 087597 where appaling carnage resulted, especially when the Germans mortared it themselves. At the end of the day it was piled high with German dead.

During all this free-lance Colonel Waddell had detached himself with the self appointed job of O.C. smoke, Tigers being suspected on the East. Now Herbert Waddell with true Scottish conservancy did not intend to waste that smoke. So, having first placed his tank for all the German world to see, in a long discussion on the air he took Roy, the gunnery king, into advisory partnership ending thus ,"Now look here young man ah don't propose to argue any further on the 'A'—just come over to my tank". An excellent plan was finally agreed and carried out by both. Roy's tank suddenly got a colossal crack from a Sherman travelling in reverse. Bonko went round to give "what for" to the driver, who looked round and found the tank commander had been shot.

Late in the evening the Squadron was released and travelled back to Cormelles where Peter rapidly got busy on the usual perquisites—a comfortable mess, an inviting house and what have you. On the next day the Squadron once more went to Secqueville but were not required and again returned to Cormelles.

On the 10th August they were spirited away under Command of 49 Division and in renewed assocoiatin with 31 Tank Brigade, being told to harbour somewhere near Cagny. The Echelon went into Grentheville, Nigel leading the Crocs to where he had proudly discovered the perfect harbour for the tanks just NW of Cagny at 097648. Two minutes later the place was being shelled by 88s. Tpr Millard and the ever cheerful Fossey were wounded here. The whole of that area was overlooked from the high ground west of Troarn and the slightest movement anywhere brought stonks down. Nigel and George spent that day in a scout car, unpleasantly exposed on skylines to 88s which had not the slightest hesitation in potting at them whenever they appeared, travelling about to various 'O' Groups. A troop was asked for to go into the rubble of Vimont—but after a Wasp was brewed by an 88 firing straight down the road, rapidly followed by a tank in the same manner, the idea was given up. Still being potted at by 88s the scout car survived next as far as Chicheboville where a plan was laid on to attack Benauville on the next day and then work up to Vimont from the south. This Nigel tied up with the 9 RTR, beautifully timing his arrival at the harbour to coincide with another hefty stonk.

During the night the Squadron moved to the woods just NE of Secqueville la Compagne. The attack in fact never did go in but the Squadron spent three most unpleasant days in these woods. Sgt Decent bowled up from Workshops during daylight with his tank and from then on the place became a very favourite spot for German shoots. Dicky Preston, the padre, came along and the tanks were formed into a crescent whilst he gave a service. It was an extraordinary thing but during that service not a single shell came over. As soon as it was over it all started up again. On the 12th of August all the best people back home began to shoot grouse. But in the woods at Secqueville the Boche was going out for different game and that day he winged five—Sgt Wetherell, Cpl Grant, Cpl Wallace, Tpr Bewsher and Tpr Walsh. On the 13th however the Squadron were put under command of 2 Canadian Corps for "Tallulah" and moved back during the night to Cormelles. The trip back lay through a colossal minefield near La Hogue, in an area bombed right off the map. In the pitch darkness Sgt Huxtable, losing sight of the Croc in front, took a gamble on a turning —he lost the toss and the way, and nearly half the Squadron followed. It was here, when they were completely lost in the desolate maze, that Davenport offered to walk in front of the column prodding all the way for mines. Fortunately at that minute a wrathful Captain Moss appeared from nowhere and led them back through the gap.

"Tallulah" was to be a repetition of "Totalise" methods in order to sieze the commanding ground North and North-East of Falaise. The famous Falaise pocket was at last in the making. 2 Canadian Corps was to attack on a two Division front with right 3 Canadian Infantry Division and left 2 Canadian Infantry Division. Again two armoured columns were to lead—right 2 Canadian Brigade, left 4 Canadian Armoured Birgade, these in turn followed by Priest-borne battalions of 9 and 8 Canadian Infantry Brigades respectively to clear the River Laison after the armour had crossed over. This time however the operation was to take place in daylight with intensive smoke on the flanks and heavy bomber support. 'B' Squadron were in support of 8 Canadian Infantry Brigade and allotted primarily to the Regiment de Chaudiere to assist if necessary in clearing Rouvres and its neighbouring chateau. H hour was noon 14 August.

On the appointed day 'B' Squadron formed up at St. Aignan de Cramesnil and after crossing the Start Line just south went flat out in tactical formation to the high ground north of Rouves, there to wait until required. Here the Crocs came in for a good deal of direct anti-tank fire from the other side of the river and a Flail brewed at the side of Tony Ward. Nigel saw the AP spurts near Tony's Croc and told him to pull back as he was being fired at. Back came the "young man's" answer, "You're telling **me**". By use of extensive smoke the Squadron managed to get into more reasonable positions. Peter claimed one anti-tank gun. First news from the infantry was that their objective was taken and cleared and that assistance was not required. The Squadron L.O., John Shearman, apprised the Brigade Commander of this. Having lost all communication with his battalion the Brigadier was pleasantly surprised more than somewhat and used the Crocodile communications to give orders to his other two battalions to advance, as he was not in touch with them either.

Late that evening the party pulled out to Garcelles Secqueville to refuel. Here old "Speedy" was doing his nut. The bombing had again partially misfired and the echelon had been caught on the fringe, fortunately without casualty. Insult had been added to injury by

41

the appearance of Spits which machine-gunned them up and down the hedgerow, again fortunately without casualty. "Look here sir, if they bastards is going to keep on a bombing of us like this how the hell am I to keep the echelon together?" But he had been lucky. That same day almost the whole of 'A' Squadron's echelon, a short distance away, had been sadly obliterated by the same "precision" bombing. Now an outbreak of flares in the sky predicted a German bombing effort and decided Nigel to carry on to Le Bras—as things turned out a very wise decision.

The Squadron was now put in Army Reserve as the whole thing swept forward. Peter of course was all for moving back lock, stock and barrel to Cormelles where the sweets of life might once more be taken firmly in hand. It was gently but no less firmly pointed out by the C.O. that the axis of advance happened to be in a totally different direction. It was plain who would win the discussion—on 20 August the Squadron moved to 159411 just SW of Epaney.

Meanwhile Lieut Mason had left and Lieut Terry Conway—"Tempo"—joined the Squadron to take over 10 Troop. Tempo had a face like a film star and an action on the dance floor which had all the suave elegance of Sylvester combined with all the meticulousness of a Harry Barrow out to make a century. His rhythmic foot rasps on some tiny spot—watch him disengage from his partner and with dainty toe kick away the offending morsel of chewing gum, compo biscuit or what have you. In action on the field just as smooth—cool, calm and imperturbable.

On the 20th August then, at seven days notice to move, 'B' Squadron took up residence in an extremely muddy field and arrangements went ahead for a "roarer" in the officer's mess which was very fortunately cancelled. For "seven day notice" or any other notice falls among those many chimera designed solely to feed the ever hungry bumf-machine, an exquisite device fashioned that there may not exist widespread unemployment in the Staff. At 0230 hrs on that same night an L.O. made a most unwelcome appearance with orders for the Squadron to move at first light to the area Les Authieux Papillon 4080 (Sheet

42

7/F4), whilst the squadron-commander with an L.O. were to report forthwith to HQ 7 Armoured Division under whose command they now came. Major Ryle and Captain Moss accordingly set off and by good fortune alone hit on the correct location of 7 Armoured Division after a very ambiguous map reference which could have referred equally to two places fifty miles apart. A wet and miserable column of tanks set out under an even more wet, grim and miserable Storrar. Not before Lieut Sander had armed himself however for the journey with an empty 75mm shell case for he was suffering more than somewhat from diaorrhea, and showing more than ever that 19th century "mal du siecle" look. "Well I mean to say old boy forty times in one day is a bit too much. Don't you agree?" For Tpr Bailey Harry had a different solution. Periodically he would drop him off and just as regularly L/C Short would retrieve him on his motor cycle, returning him to Harry. For the tracks must keep rolling.

Beyond St Pierre the column was stopped by a very irate DAQMG of the Highland Division who informed George that he knew nothing of the Crocs, wanted nothing of the Crocs and would the Crocs damn well get off his axis or else. Well George is a Scotsman too and in best Gaelic English retorted it would be a pleasure, or something to that effect, and pulled into an orchard at 296510 NE of St. Pierre Sur Dives. Nigel burst into this serene atmosphere from 7 Armoured Division with the news that the Squadron's move was a mistake anyway. True they had a vague recollection of a passing mention some few days ago that the Crocs would have been useful on a certain strong-point but that was all over and done with long ago. Sorry and all that. George's language is a little strong at times. But that night he left "B" Squadron to rejoin his beloved 'A'. That night too the then Lieut Harry Cobden joined the Squadron and took over the job of Recce Officer. Harry had made a good job of the Recce Troop before the Regiment came over here and lost it. He had then spent some time with 'C' and had lately been letting himself go at Tac HQ, where he had stepped up the personnel to something like fifteen, forcing Colonel Waddell to split off once more into a sort of Tac Tac HQ. He had a jeep which he drove with considerable skill and

43

considerable speed, and could sit a horse outside the Palace Gates.

7th Armoured Division were making a concerted drive east through Lisieux and 'B' Squadron were kept in reserve to deal with stubborn pockets that might crop up, moving on the 23rd to 442786 and thence to 506680 (7/F4) just SW of Lisieux. But the advance along the whole front was now proceeding at a pace which made it impossible for the Crocs to keep up and be put into operation against any strongpoint before it was quickly reduced by normal arms alone.

Eastwards and ever East. Past the roadside havoc that had been a German Army. The dead horses by the road, the long lines packed tight with overturned and burnt out trucks, guns and tanks, the river valleys choc full of the German impedimenta of war.

On the 27th the Squadron came under command of 33 Armoured Brigade, a very favourite one, and moved just west of St Georges de Bierbe with a view to helping on the River Risle. Again however not required and so on to 965032 this time with eyes on that landmark the Seine. On the 29th once more on the move to 985077 (8E/6) just north of Bourg Achard with a view to crossing the Seine. Here the Squadron liberally endowed itself with high-powerd German motor cars and other things conducive not only to a pleasant life but operational efficiency as well, which later higher authority saw fit to take away. Remember that other "Speedy" Bill Crouch, the old Chev that went to Brest and back and got the bread to Knocke when all else failed ? If you don't Bob Albany does— used up his two days short leave getting it to the Brussels dump. But later it looked so nice in that window with the handsome price ticket attached.

Into this equestrian and pastoral world of prosperity, and war as it might be, out of the blue came the thunderbolt. 'B' Squadron had been detailed by some mysterious power to join the Americans in front of Brest, and moreover would proceed forthwith. The Colonel knew nothing about it, the Brigadier very little else. The Squadron was in fact expecting a long overdue overhaul and Rest Camp. But there it was—very tasty, very sweet. Good grub, an experience and lots of other things besides.

44

No, 'B' Squadron certainly weren't saying anything about it. On the 7th September Peck mounted his horse for the last time, and Nigel gave a final expert milking to the Squadron cow. That evening the transporters roared into life and 'B' Squadron was off, taking in tow 16 Platoon of 502 RASC Company and a Medical Section of the 31 Tank Brigade Light Field Ambulance.

To John Teasdale and John East of the RASC the Squadron owes a lot and here gratefully acknowledges their long association with 16 Platoon which has always done them proud, and not only at Brest. Ask John Teasdale and John East for a large ration of the impossible and they'd say, "Send you some up tomorrow, old boy, with the petrol." And they did.

With the Light Field Ambulance came Lieut Harbinson and for a time Lt-Col. Hutchinson, that incredible phenomenon of medicoes. Of the most secret American counsels of war he would say, "Not a man there below a general, old boy, except me of course".

En route the Squadron picked up several notables. Lieut Cliff Shone of all people—"Permission to pan him Major !" Cliff never stopped laughing at life. Whether his tank brewed or whether he'd had the most God-awful blind the night before he'd still come out smiling. Bags of common sense too. He would go on drinking and arguing till he fell asleep. And without exception his first question would be "wheres me tuth?" God knows in what queer places we found that solitary tooth-anywhere from a ships lavatory to a forest clearing, but find it we always did—had to, or the show couldn't go on. Peter and Cliff were as thick as thieves—and the combination approximated to a hurricane. Lieut Hare who took over John Shearman's tank at Brest and had the luckiest escape of any man. Cpl. Gilbert.

TO:- Major Nigel Ryle,
   Commanding 'B' Squadron,

   141st Regiment,
    Royal Armoured Corps
        (The Buffs),

THRU:- Commanding General,
   12th Army Group.

 1. I desire to commend you and the members of your command for the superior service while serving with this Division during the final stages of the siege on the Fortress Brest, France, September 1944.

 2. Upon attachment to this Division your Squadron conducted an intensive training programme with the infantry battalions of the 116th Infantry, then entered into combat and elements of your command were instrumental in the reduction of Fort Montbarey, a very difficult task. Your troops continued to perform most creditably with this regiment, and also the 115th Infantry and the 5th Ranger Battalion. Troops of this Division were always most enthusiastic as to your combat efficiency.

    C. H. GERHARDT,
   Major General U.S. Army,
     Commanding.

YANKEE DOODLE

The journey there was pleasant enough. The air of liberation was still abroad. True the flowers had given out, but the onions pelted at the passing column had if anything a sweeter smell. Takes a deal of beating an onion, taken raw maybe for elevenses with a mite of cheese or whopped whole into a rabbit stew.

Now westwards and all the time westwards. Bernay, Alencon, Domfront, Mayenne, Fougeres, Rennes, Dinon, St. Brieue, Morlaix. These are something which Harry Barrow wouldn't know for he has a mind that it was damned good drinking all the way. But four hundred miles is a tidy trek for Diamond T's and they were soon straggled all along that route, fifty miles north and fifty miles south of it too with Tony whipping them in.

Le Folgeat is some eight miles N.N.E. of Brest and on the 7th Nigel and Harry Cobden, standing in the harbour there, could only welcome five Crocs in. Nevertheless by late afternoon of the 8th the last straggler was roaring in and the Squadron was hard down to it preparing for action. Work before play. Brest had to be liquidated and that quickly. A great U-Boat base and a formidable garrison it formed a distinct menace and tied down forces which could ill be spared. And the Allies were thirsting for ports.

Nigel and Harry Cobden had already been recceing the best possible country over which to employ the Crocs and it wasn't too promising. Here was bocage at its very worst—minute fields bounded by banks 8—10 feet high and the same width. A few days later Nigel and the Americans were to get down in real earnest to this problem but meanwhile on the 8th itself, under command of U.S. 157 Regiment, the Squadron moved to an area at Bour-Blanc. Thence with the 1st Battalion to the outskirts of Lambezelec, where pressure from the doughboys had driven the Germans into the main fortifications. Here the defences were well-nigh impregnable, situated as they were behind a colossal minefield, a moat 40 feet wide and 20 feet deep, then a wall some 60 feet high banked on the German side with earth to distance of 80-100 feet. The whole area in front covered by guns and mortars of every type and calibre—15 cm hows, hordes of 88s, 40mms, 20 mms and dozens of just plain ordinary M.G.s In one of the recces you could see Jerry setting up yet another 88. A tank destroyer had a crack and missed badly—Harry Barrow did his nut.

Nevertheless after several very detailed recces under the enemy's nose and fire a plan was eventually hammered out. On the left Nigel aimed to attack due south with Harry Cobden and Peter over a distance of some 350 yards, supported by a company of Shermans, five M10s, several 240mms and a company of 155mm S.Ps. On the right Roy Moss aimed to do the same with Tony from N.E. to S.W. A conspicuous feature of the operation throughout was the absence of wholesale artillery such as the Squadron had become accustomed to with the British Army—here you had to act as your own. Listening once for the sound of what had been described as a great barrage nothing more was heard than the very occasional thump of a 240 mm which would nevertheless evoke from the doughboys, "Gees, now just hark at them there guns a-popping".

Such artillery as there was on this occasion was designed to breach the wall by direct fire from the 240mms covered by smoke and H.E. from the 155s. An all-out assault by the Crocs would then flame the gun positions and pillboxes on and in front of the wall, whereupon the infantry would be launched through a corridor of flame into the breach to a *sauve qui peut*.

At the appointed hour the Crocs rolled to a standstill and switched off behind a small hill some 300 yards short of the fort, then watched from ringside seats the extraordinary spectacle of a great 240mm in full view pounding away at the fort from a mere 100 yards. When assigned this somewhat unorthodox task the officer in charge of the guns had remarked "Gees, guess it's going to be mighty tough sitting out there like that." Which merely evoked the laconic reply "So what ! Guess you got spare crews ain't you". All day long it pounded away, the crews

48

taking one hell of a packet. But did it make the slightest dent?—did it hell!

After two days the whole show was declared off in favour of an entirely new approach on Brest. On the 12th of September the Crocs pulled out and clocked fifty miles to Loc Maria, joining up with the 29th U.S. Infantry Div who were attacking Recouvrances (the western and most important half of Brest, holding as it did the giant submarine pens) from the west. Fort Montbarey, key to the defences, barred the way.

29 Div was for 'B' Squadron a superb impresssion of the American Army, the "Let's Go" boys were the sort of guys with whom you were proud to scrap. Texan Major Dallas, commanding 1st Battalion 116 Regiment, toting his 45 around and drawling out to Nigel way up in front of Fort Montbarey on a recce, "Guess you and I Major will just stand up here a while and draw a little fire, just find out where them goddam machine guns is firing from." One of the few, so very few, absolutely fearless men who can stand unperturbed in a hail of bullets and mortar fire and bear a life that is doubly charmed. Dallas never gave out the location of his command post. It was invariably with the leading platoon—himself, a runner and a guy with a telephone. "Guess then if folks really want to see me well they'll come and see me." We hand it to Major Dallas in a big way. General Gerhard commanding the Division, wining and dining Nigel. Up against Fort Montbarey in a sticky passage he rang up Dallas, as usual with the leading platoon, and Nigel with Dallas heard this, "Just want a word with you Dallas so I guess I'll be on my way right now to see you." "Well sir its mighty hot right here now. Don't kinda recommend it." "Why, say, I guess we're all expendable aint we?" Colonel Wilson, his second in command, a grand old southern gentleman with old-world courtesy and kindness, making a great fuss of the Playboys and saying they must have more cigarettes. And the doughboys. Sgt Humphrey, engineer, with damn near every medal America has to offer including the Congressional Medal of Honour, Doing hair-raising recces, clearing paths through the minefields in broad daylight the whole way along for the the Crocs, and escaping in some miraculous way with his

49

own life though his men were falling right, left and centre all round. The wireless operator who rolled up to attach himself to Nigel. "What's your name?" asked Nigel. "Why Major just call me Tony an' ah'll be right up your arse". And as the recce parties crawled past the forward slits without exception the men manning them would stand up and salute. "Morning Cap," or "Morning Major."

Right away Nigel and 29 Div got down to the technical and tactical problems of the Crocodiles in this bocage stuff. On the technical side there resulted the astonishing feat of designing, making and fitting a Rhinocerous type hedgecutter to every tank within three days. Drive, enthusiasm, and the superiority of services which manpower helped to give them. Not one welder but two whole teams working 24 hours long by shifts. "Let's Go". On the tactical side the same drive from both sides. Here the problem was both general and particular. The Americans had little experience of close co-operation with tanks, and none with flamethrowers. It was virgin ground for those general principles dearly bought in the bridgehead. In particular how to apply them over this extraordinary ground. Nigel and the Americam staff hammered away and produced the drill, then down to training in real earnest.

Meanwhile too recces and planning were going on with the 1st Battalion for Fort Montbarey, the whole success of the operation being in large measure due to the detailed manner in which these were executed. Every recce brought down heavy fire from mortars and 40mms firing direct, but time after time the Croc recce groups got away with it. Nigel and Harry Cobden in particular were responsible for some very hair-raising recces. For the problem of getting Crocs within flaming range of the objective was anything but simple, the outer defences of the dominating fort being extremely strong. First a colossal minefield of deadly 300 lb. naval shells running in front of the defences in a continuous line N.E. to Fort Keranroux and beyond. Against these, even had there been any, Flails would have been blown sky-high. It meant therefore a painfully slow and expensive path-clearing effort by the sappers, relying mainly on the guns of the tanks to protect them. After that a wide anti-tank ditch, with no AVREs to lay bridges. Then three lines of defence heavily defended by M.Gs, 40mms and 20mms, many in pill-boxes. The whole of this area was so cratered to hell as to be almost impassable by ordinary tanks never mind Crocs. Finally the kernel of the position, the fort itself, hedged in by sunken roads, surrounded by a moat forty feet wide and twenty feet deep and walls so loopholed that the garrision could fire into the moat from either side.

And now it was all set to go. On the night of the 13th September, masked by artillery fire, the Crocs were crawling up to the Start Line at a mere 2 m.p.h. ready to go in next day. First light found the four HQ tanks and a platoon of M10s, guns blazing away all out, covering an assault company of infantry as they secured a footing on the anti-tank ditch. In the wake of the infantry with superb courage the engineers were clearing a path through the minefield and carrying forward prepared charges for the ditch. Casualties were high but they carried on. By midday this phase was complete. The assault infantry had penetrated within about 200 yards of the fort but were now completely stopped and pinned down. The time had come to put in the "young man" with 8 Troop to wipe out the outer defence north and north east of the fort. Captain Cobden made a plan with the reserve company but first had to go on foot with Sgt Humphreys as far as the anti-tank ditch to check a possible crossing. He found one spot and one only where it was just feasible that a Croc might go and only just—a fortuitous conjunction of craters that had torn down the walls. Though a heavy toll was taken of the sappers, Humphreys and Harry somehow made it there and back. Very creditable. At 1400 hrs 8 Troop and its attendant gun tanks rolled into action and Tony, ably assisted by the superb driving of Tpr Clare, was already winning his Silver Star.

As the column headed through the minefield—Tony, "Dinnah" Briggs, Harry Cobden and Lt. Hare in that order—Roy and Nigel opened up again with the three M10s. Tony was making the grade O.K., daintily picking his way through the craters within the limits of the cleared path and firing as he went. But Jake Morley's luck was right out. A 300 lb. shell had been overlooked and his track touched it off with most fearsome results. There was a colossal explosion and the whole track wrapped itself over the turret. The driver, L/C Moore, was killed outright. Jake Morley, Tpr Thorne, Adams and Worth where hellishly battered and spent many months in hospital—Thorne and Worthy having both legs broken amongst other things.

This completely blocked the whole column behind. Roy and Nigel were stepping up their guns and the M10s filling in as the engineers began desperately clearing a further passage round the dead Croc.

But Tony was going strong. Through the minefield and on to the tricky anti-tank ditch, over it by the skin of his tracks, then a very pretty game of in and out the craters, scything his burning track of death through the rich harvest of MGs and light A.A./AT guns. Driving and commanding were and had to be superb. The infantry were following up and a steady stream of prisoners now flowed back. Right up to the sunken road on the north side, from where he flamed and shot the infantry into the German positions along the whole length of the wood surrounding the fort. Then over to the left and round the corner, flaming and blasting until the doughboys were in possession of the eastern wooded fringe as well— drill working famously, infantry right up behind and cashing in one hundred per cent. Tony got "proper mad" at a 50mm firing hard at him from a pillbox where the sunken road meets the main road and sent a 75mm crashing through the slit into the ammunition inside. The top blew right off and with fragments of the crew sailed way up. Another 50mm firing from the S.E. never recovered from the same medicine.

It now looked as if the fort itself would fall and Tony asked to do a chukka down S.E. towards the houses skirting Recouvrances. He stormed off some 900 yards, using up all his H.E. and 20 belts of Besa. Disdainfully giving the K.O. to a 10.5cm field gun and its crew he was flinging stuff at everything rash enough to show its head, finally coming to the houses and giving them a look of glaring derision. The infantry however had not left the area of the fort and Tony now considered he'd had sufficient outing. Turning round he headed back to the southern edge of the.fort. Some two hundred yards from it he was somewhat perturbed when the Croc suddenly heeled over on its side and crashed down a bunker full of Germans. White flags momentarily appeared and just as rapidly disappeared as they realised the entry was unrehearsed. Tony shut down quickly to have a quiet think. This wasn't helped any by the pair of steel blue eyes which tried to peer at him through the periscope, and a one sided staring match now began. "Oh Jerry what big eyes you've got". Tony dialled Whitehall 1212 and gave Nigel the dope. No acknowledgement came through and Tony went on chattering away amiably to himself—the Germans, crafty sods, had whipped his aerial. Further complications now set in—the tilt of the tank was forcing the petrol out and fumes were filling the tank. Worse still the fall had released a methyl-bromide extinguisher inside the tank and this was now discharging at full speed. One by one the crew were starting to pass out and Tony felt more than ever that without a breath of fresh air life just wasn't on. So what does the brave little lad do but pop his revolver out of the hatch, quickly follows with his head and in best Yorkshire German yells "Hande hoch". At which unexpected display of awfully bad behaviour—but then Tony never excelled in the drawing roon—the Germans duly hoched their hands. Before they could recover their sang froid the rest of the crew were already out, and Tony making a grab at the Bren was testing it with fearsome abandon. So the Germans lined up, all thirty nine.

Meanwhile, unbeknown to Tony, his first message **had** got through and Nigel had tackled Major Dallas about it. Well Dallas said he'd get that crew out if it was the last thing he did and mustered all the guys he had left with him—some engineers, jeep drivers and cooks. This motley force had got to within 200 yards of Tony but there they were stopped by machine gun fire from the fortress. As they lay prostrate to work this one out the whole thing solved itself before their eyes. Now Tony runs in his spare time and what he can do he doesn't see why others shouldn't. So now he said something in German which meant "scram" and sounded like nothing on earth, setting the whole column off at the double for the eastern edge of the fort and brandishing the Bren for all he was worth. German machine guns immediately started to smarten the party up but that only got the journey over more quickly and there they were at last in the hands of the rescue party. Tony stuck around with them to quieter regions where they were searched by other Americans. 8 Troop looked particularly scruffy that day and one can well sympathise with the guy who said "Guess we'd better search these guys too." Then got a piece of Tony's mind.

Another rescue force was also on its way. Slowly following the straggling tape line of the Sappers Cpl Briggs finally burst through the minefield up to the N.W. corner of the fort where he dismounted to look for Tony's tracks, Tony's Croc now being out of sight. Here he was inveigled into a little private war of some American officer and had just completed a very unpleasant recce some thirty yards from the Germans when Captain Cobden bowled up and took him on another, again to look for Tony's tracks which were duly found. Off set the column again, rounding the first corner. Then—oh my, poor guy —Cpl Briggs dropped himself well and truly in the, well in the mire. His Croc capsized into a concealed cesspool, tilted over until the foul stuff was lapping round the turret. At which precise moment Harry Cobden's tank went off its tracks and Lieut Hare went down a crater. Whilst Sgt Norrington got Harry's tank back on its tracks Harry ran over to Cpl Briggs, and together they tried to work out a solution. This wasn't too simple with 40mms and 20 mms sniping them the whole time from the fortress. However Lieut Hare had now extricated his tank and whilst Harry went over to contact Tony, who was just coming in, Cpl Briggs dodged in and out of the 40mms making frantic visual signals to Lieut Hare's tank. It was five minutes before there was any response and the tank came over. Cpl Briggs got the Bren out and covered the driver and co-driver, Tpr Neale and Tpr Jolly, whilst with sleeves rolled up they plunged deep into the liquid excrement, "eyes down, look in", and hooked up the tow-rope. And that's how 8 Troop got it's present name.

Harry Cobden, tank bedecked with prisoners, now

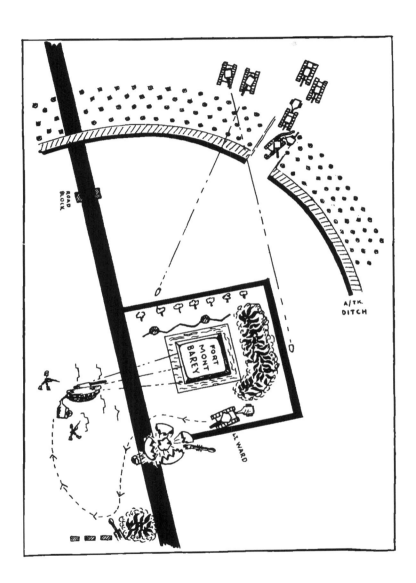

ROAD BLOCK

A/TK. DITCH

FORT MONT BAREY

Lt WARD

55

56

PLAYBOYS AT BREST.

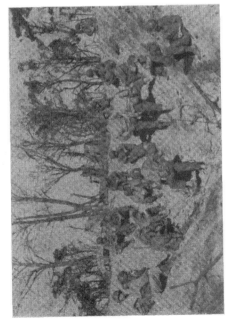

57

IN ACTION AT BREST.

58

led the tiny cortege back. Both he and Cpl Briggs safely navigated the treacherous minefield gap but Lt. Hare touched off a further 300 lb. shell in another terrific explosion. Followed the awful sight of a great Churchill turret flying through the air. The driver, Tpr Guy, was killed outright. The co-driver, Tpr Frudd, died the next day. The turret crew had the most amazing escapes. Blown out with the turret they fell out in mid-air and by the grace of God landed in a different spot— Lt Hare, Sgt Cowe and L/C Raymond. Badly battered, with smashed ankles and other injuries, they nevertheless survived. L/C Raymond with a broken thigh was as cool as any cucumber as they picked him up.

6 officers and 116 O.Rs taken prisoner, several guns knocked out, a hell of a lot killed, a hell of a lot put to flight and a daring penetration to Recouvrances. Not bad for a lone Croc, in fact probably a record.

The fortress itself refused to capitulate and once more Dallas and Nigel got their heads together. First thing Nigel insisted on the minefield gap being completely cleared and approaches bulldozed to the fortress. This took up the greater portion of next day whilst the three remaining H.Q tanks whiled away the time by plastering up the fort. At the same time complete recces up to the edge of the moat were made, each Croc commander taking a good peek at the ground.

On the morning of the 16th Nigel went forward to Major Dallas's command post, some fifty yards from the fort itself, whilst Roy brought up 9 Troop commanded on this occasion by Sgt Decent. They fanned out on the norther side at the edge of the moat and sent 75s and 95s crashing into the fort. The troop emptied its trailers in the moat and across the other side in one glorious conflagration of flame and smoke. Then from a shelter in the moat emerged "Hermann the German". Dallas sent him back into the fort to demand its surrender at the pistol point. But that modernised mediaeval fort was just as tough as ever. Out came "Hermann the German" to tell Dallas that the commandant's orders were to remain there and fight to the bitter end—and unless they produced a damn sight more flame and destruction so he would. You know the idea, "C'est dommage mais—

nous sommes soldats". There could of course be only one reaction. "He wants it, well we've got it". Terry came in with 10 Troop and used up the whole of his H.E and flame in one mad outburst, quickly replaced by Cliff with 6 Troop who piled in just as heavy. At the same time all available fire power, infantry mortars, phosphorus shells and heavy weapons crashed down. Two 105mm close-support Hows lined up into action against the gate itself, Roy pounding away with them. The outhouses were now a blazing inferno and a truly Walt Disney nighmare of flame, smoke, flying metal, sound and fury. Gradually the weight shifted its point of impact as a task force of infantry jumped into the moat and placed charges against the wall. The little force returned and blew the charges. Straightway into the hole charged the infantry covered by an absolute crescendo of flame, 75s, Besa and smoke. Cliff was even using up his hand smoke grenades Straight through the outhouses, capturing en route 30 P.W. too asphyxiated by the flame and smoke to surrender. A sharp spell of hand-to-hand fighting and the show was over, the remainder of the garrison left alive surrendering—78 O.Rs, 3 Officers, a W.O. and an officer cadet.

In this later stage Roy had been wounded in the arm, but continued to fire his tank until carried out through loss of blood and evacuated to hospital—not before Stroud, cooking a meal some way back, had forced him to have his dinner. Knowing Roy it wouldn't take all that much forcing.

Montbarey spelt the end of the 30,000 garrison in Brest. A great breach had been torn through their main fortifications and the Americans were now able to infiltrate successfully.Into Recouvrances the very next day sailed Captain Cobden and Harry Barrow to plan a battle inside Brest itself with the 115 Infantry Regiment and Nigel with the 5th Rangers. Once more the same thorough recces and plans, and everything was lined up to go on the 18th. But now the whole thing began to crumble and the Germans packed in here without waiting for the Crocs. For one more day the Crocs stood by, largely employed now in watching the fascinating American system of search. "All cameras this way". Mitch stumbled over a payroll which was divided up amongst the Squadron. And as the last P.W. rolled in Cliff settled down with the Americans to the blind of his life—unconscious and happy they tucked him into the co-drivers seat and took him home. Taxi !

Two days more were spent in recovery and salvage before the Playboys were once more under way for Lesneven, there to await transporters.

Tony got the Silver Star and was henceforth suspected of signing all his letters Tony Ward, S.S. Nigel, Roy Moss, Lieut Hare, Clare, Harris Lynn, Parry, Jake Morley, Thorne, Adams and Worthy, Sgt Cowe (what tremendous meals he cooked) and L/C Raymond—all these earned the Bronze Star. For those who were still able to campaign dear old Monica, Roy's wife, provided the first temporary ribbons. Praises were heaped high on the Squadron right up to SHAEF and momentous reports made on their efforts. Above all "Life" featured them. This is the tail end of one report from the 12th U.S. Army approved by General Simpson and subsequently by Monty through Guingand :

4. CONCLUSIONS

The flamethrower tanks were a very important factor in the capture of Fort Montbarey. Their successful use in this operation can be attributed to the following factors.

(1). The splendid co-operation between the infantry battalion commander and Major Ryle, the flamethrower Squadron Commander, and the great pains which they took in recce and detailed planning for the operation.

(2). The great courage displayed by the British flamethrower unit and the American infantry which took part in this attack.

(3). The skilful employment of the flamethrower effectively upon the vulnerable parts of the fort. Also the effective use of their 75mm gun and machine guns against the enemy in the Fort and outlying positions.

5. RECOMMENDATIONS.

It is believed that the flamethrower tank has a very definite usfulness in support of the infantry in hedgerow or similar country where the terrain is favourable to the enemy in defence but where it will permit operation of the tanks. Also where the infantry is confronted with defensive installations which can be attached effectively by the flames such as were found at Fort Montbarey. It is believed that one or two battalions of these flame-throwers tanks might well be assigned to the Army and held as troops for employment where needed''.

Back in the field of Le Folgeat the Playboys went to town in their own inimitable style—elementary my dear Watson, ssh ! Redites moi ces choses tendres. And with Brest just behind them there was little shortage of wine and the finer things of life. High light was the F.F.I. dinner in which Tony reached his greatest height of virtue ever, getting roaring tight. Staggering out through the corridor of applauding and charming mesdames and mesdamoiselles he fell headlong on terra firma and, like any drowning man clutching for a straw, heaved himself upright again by the simple and almost disastrous expedient of hanging on their skirts. Another was the football match with Lesneven in which the Playboys were well and truly trounced 12-1 and Nigel was presented, by a charming little filly, with a great bouquet. Nigel and the other officers in fact weren't losing any time. Every night a glorious dash to Morlaix or any other place that offered wine, fun and games until the early hours. Cliff and Peter like a junior tornado. Lobsters, steaks, Hotel de Force—ah, voila quelquechose. Nigel had dinner with General Gerhardt and received his decoration, then broadcast with the General on the B.B.C., landing home with the milk as merry as a cricket. Mind you Nigel on occasions can suffer from illusions. On one such evening he was adamant that a 15 cwt was functionally the same as any Rhinocerous hedge-cutter. He tore round the field making passes at the banks and at the speed he went he nearly made it too.

News came at last that the Playboys would make the trip by sea and they duly moved to St Michel on the 28th. It was too much to hope yet—but the Playboys star was getting brighter. Cliff boarded one of the two LSTs with Mitchell to get the dope and both were promptly ushered into the ward room. "Mr. Shone and Mr. Mitchell". "Nice being an officer for half an hour," said Mitch as they emerged replete. Next morning half the echelon embarked but the remainder had to wait until the evening. They were called forward too early after the tide and within minutes the beach was littered in bogged trucks. The German ten-tonner sank in over the top. Peter was driving the spare jeep in the dark with a hilarious crowd of Cliff, Harry Barrow and Tony Ward. "Make towards that light and you'll be O.K." said someone. Next minute the jeep was completely submerged in salt water and four forlorn figures were standing in the radiator in the smallest desert island out. Laugh !

On the 30th the ships set sail and the bottles were produced. Cliff did another sleepy blackout in the most extraordinary retreat and the Doc was plaintively taxing Roy, "Come and see Cliff. We must **do** something. We must **do** something". But all Roy could get out of Cliff was, "I've lost mi tuth". Roy found his tooth for him. The men on Cpl Briggs' ship were getting into bad odour with the skipper who accused them of urinating down the side, little knowing the vicissitudes of Cpl Briggs tank.

Sunday morning found them in the Solent looking at England—so near and yet so far. This was hell as the L.S.Ts shifted their positions up and down—dare they hope to make it. But one L.S.T. needed repairs and the other wouldn't sail alone. As soon as his ship weighed anchor Nigel was over the side in a boat and on shore like a stroke of lightning pulling strings, drinking a dirty pint and doing everything he knew. He returned late in the evening and announced that they would go ashore next moring for 24 hrs. More bottles came out. Nigel had done it again. Cpl Kessell and L/C Ruth got down to work, performing miracles in the way of requisite lists, addresses, pay etc., and the next norning the Squadron went ashore to be rushed off in lorries to the barracks. Here Nigel announced that they would now get 48 hrs. More cheers. More bottles. More work for Kessell and Ruth—churning out passes, ration books and God knows what. Nigel trying to get off the long distance chaps first, troop commanders trying to pull fast ones for their troops. At 1140 Cpl Kessel and L/C Ruth were the last to leave, with twenty minutes in which to catch their train. They made it.

For this after all was the high light of the Brest campaign. England, wives, mothers, families and homes. Here is something into which we will not intrude.

And on Wednesday evening not a single chap who failed to turn up once again at the barracks. Not even Nigel. But one Playboy as he approached the gate was greeted by two delightful ladies asking him the whereabouts of Nigel Ryle. No Cpl Russell, Major Ryle did *not* spend the night amongst those barrack buildings.

THE SCHELDT POCKET

On the 6th October the Playboys once more touched down on the continent, this time at Ostend, sadly depleted in AFVs and personnel and expecting a thorough overhaul and refit. One HQ tank and one Croc had been completely written off at Brest, another derelict was abandoned on the quay at Ostend. The rest were almost on the thousand mark without overhaul and dying of old age and lack of spares during the spell at Brest.

But it was not to be. Antwerp had been liberated, but the approaches were still controlled by the guns of the German forts along the Scheldt. With supply lines stretching right back to Bayeux every day was important. 3 Canadian Division were slowly clearing up the Scheldt pocket, but after heavy casualties and with no armour of their own were screaming for funnies.

So after two glorious days in the luxury hotels of Blankenburg, reading the 24 bags of mail which had never reached them at Brest and indulging in more colourful activities, the Squadron moved to Knesselaere, there to patch up major repair jobs from its own resources and get fit to fight as best it could. Here George Storrer came along for another spell, Captain Cobden and Captain Shearman leaving for RHQ and 'C' Squadron respectively.

Any spare time was certainly not wasted with Bruges so close at hand. Peter had his business and relatives there. Well if you must have things like that in Bruges and Dicky happens to be your very pretty cousin with some very jolie friends then you must lay on a party— and Peter laid on two. It says much for these parties that at the end of one Peter was assiduously putting tomatoes through the coffee grinder, in another Nigel was carried out completely flat and George was most definitely making passes at Susette.

However on the 16th October the move order arrived at last and next day the Squadron was on its way to a farm near the little Dutch village of Biervliet, in support of 9 Canadian Brigade to clear up Breskens. Harry Barrow, in charge of one block, did his nut when a passer-by said yes he'd seen some Churchills up the road all brewing up in flames. However it turned out to be a luckless Squadron of AVREs, one of whose tanks had exploded and set off the others, crammed full of explosives, by sympathetic detonation, killing or wounding most people in the Squadron. That night in the rain and mud of Biervliet Colonel Waddell paid his last visit to the Squadron, leaving Captain Harry Bailey, whose one and only claim to fame was that he had officered that brilliant 8 Troop of the Eastbourne days. On a bale of straw in a bottle of gin his advent was appropriately mourned.

In retrospect the Playboys always laughed at the concluding phases of the Scheldt pocket. But as morale builders and sceptics they appreciably affected the speeding up of the securing of the Antwerp approaches. If your brigade front is the width of a single road and right at the head is a platoon that cannot move then the smallest action which enables them to get mobile again does assume some importance. On the surface it wasn't so funny for armour. In flat open country the whole area was flooded and there simply was no means of getting off the skylined dykes. Flank and front were just wide open. There was little artillery, none that could be readily spared for smoke, and no supporting armour. Not that armour could have given much support. It was just a matter of going single file up dykes so narrow that for a Crocodile to turn meant going up as far as the next transverse. If the leading tank were hit or struck a mine then the whole axis was blocked not only for the tanks but for the infantry as well, a serious proposition to be weighed when the whole advance was confined to several fingers going up the dykes. Mines were on the road in profusion and, although on the surface, the infantry could not move them in the day because they had no cover. Intelligence invariably, though often wrongly, gave the opposition as being very strong. It was a soul destroying task too knocking places to hell which sheltered sometimes Dutch civilians as well as German soldiers.

The general situation was that 9th Canadian Infantry Brigade had by the 17th October established themselves on a general line running roughly from Hoofdplaat, Ijzzendyke, St. Kruis and Ede. Orders had been received that Breskens must be cleared at once, the navy stating that if Breskens were cleared they were prepared to risk the guns from Flushing and begin to sweep the Scheldt Estuary. Information about the enemy was very vague.

It was estimated that roughly one battalion formed the garrison and Fort Frederick Henry was known to have a certain number of 20mms and two 88s. There was only one route into the town, the sea dyke being impassable. On the inland road there was a road block just south of the town—the SD & G Highlanders were first to capture this and the Crocs would then go into the town.

The Crocs therefore assembled at 146152 and Nigel went up to Battalion HQ. The infantry, somewhat surprised, reached the road block with no difficulty but got smartened up pretty quickly by a 20mm from the west when they tried to blow it with charges. It was decided to wait until nighfall. The road block was duly blown and at first light the Croc recce party arrived in the town, where the infantry were now fairly established in the southern edge and everyone was taking time off for a snooze. A fairly thorough recce was made of the whole town. There didn't seem much sign of occupation. However it was felt that a certain amount of opposition might be experienced from the North and West and it was decided that 7 Troop with Nigel should go through the town with one company clearing SW from the road junction at 094190, 6 Troop with George Storrer supporting another company by fire alone into pillboxes along the mole to the NE.

Terry Conway had brought the Crocs up meanwhile, and as the recce party joined them one of the heaviest concentrations used in the operation went down on a town unoccupied by Dutch, Germans or Allied. The column set off with Harry Barrow leading. Sgt Brandi was doing a modest 2mph on three cylinders. Just through the road block Harry dismounted to investigate the delay, jumped back in his tank and went straight down a crater damn near as big as a dining hall. The mud was so deep that it forced the flame pintle back and the Croc was soon basking in a sea of fuel. Harry changed over with Sgt Maddock and carried on down the main road running SW.

A suspicious looking blockhouse first claimed attention. It wasn't acting suspiciously and for that matter it wasn't doing any harm to anyone—but it just had that look. So Harry was prevailed upon to fill it with flame, and he wasn't sparing either. Still no smell of roast Hun issued forth and it was therefore assumed that all base suspicions were unfounded. No further resistance was met until they reached the edge of the town. The infantry then came under spandau fire from a house, but a few well directed squirts silenced this. Sgt Brandi's tracks now came off, leaving Harry and Nigel to carry on. Another 200 yds. and the party again came under fire, this time from 20mms too far away to flame—however Nigel and Harry gave supporting fire whilst an infantry platoon attacked from the right. This was quite successful and about 20 P.Ws. were taken. Further resistance came only from snipers but a few well directed squirts of flame soon settled them. Meanwhile George and Cliff fired a few desultory shots along the mole but upwards of 30 prisoners came out without showing fight, and the infantry just walked in as Peter arrived with the bread and mail. The headlines were wonderful.

After standing by all day on the 20th the Crocs returned to Hoofplaatz with the echelon and the crews fixed themselves up in the derelict shell-smashed houses. Here Tester, the major's long standing batman, was brutally and mysteriously battered into unconciousness one night and was fortunate ever to survive at all—no clue as to his assailant was ever found. Sharples, ditinguished colonel of the 85th, now took over the mess staff.

10 Troop were standing by under Terry Conway for immediate action and on the 21st Nigel and Harry Bailey chased off after an urgent call to Schoondyke to recce two positions from which the infantry had reported strong opposition. Strolling up to the forward Canadian position, some ten yards from the German one (no applause— they didn't know it), they were just in time to see a Canadian adroitly pitch a grenade right inside the German trenches. Out came 30 prisoners—poor types

and no cameras. Very gratifying and probably accounts for the temerity of the next scene. The second was a farmhouse just outside the town. The approach to it was a short distance down a long straight road stretching into an infinity of potential German machine gun positions, then turn left alongside a broad stream some 200 yards in full view. Up to the turn-off a little breathlessly—and not a shot came down that road. All that slinking for nothing—tut! "There it is," said the company commander pointing out the farmhouse. "Oh yes I think we can do that for you" said Nigel. No sign of movement. "Say you guys just stick around here and keep us covered while we have a look-see", this to the accompanying patrol. Well all you could do was just walk along like a pig-tail of schoolgirls out for the afternoon walk—but dammit you mustn't be outdone by the infantry, what! So when two Germans appeared on the other side of the stream it was nice knowing them, because they only wanted to surrender. Nearer and nearer to the house. Then out they came, hands raised—six of them—six friendly Dutch occupants. So that was

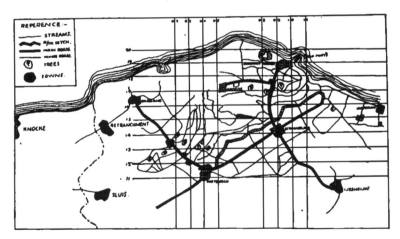

that, except for the apples and the onions carefully carried back for the rabbit stew. Mitch, who had an irresistable charm with P.Ws., had meantime been busying himself procuring for the Major and himself a nifty line in chokers. The advance went on.

Fort Frederick Henry, just NNW of Breskens, was next in the picture. The fort itself and the ground all round was so badly flooded and cratered from heavy bombing that the remains of a company who had managed to get in there and get back said that tanks could never hope to get there. On the 22nd therefore, clustered round the white mackintoshed figure of that superb Canadian Soldier, Lt Col. Forbes, a largeish party stood blatantly on the fringe of Breskens to study the problem of the fort some 800 yards away. Overhead every now and then the slow rumble and whoosh of a CPR express as the colossal shells from Flushing generously travelled on another thousand yards. Here, in collaboration with Major Ackroyd of 'B' Squadron 22 Dragoons a plan was made for all the Crocs and all the flails to put over a hefty stonk from here and shoot the infantry in, changing targets in response to light signals and wireless control. George Storrer sorted out fire positions for everybody and in the middle of the night Tony Ward was sent off to get 2000 extra rounds of 75. This was going to be some shoot. On the 23rd, in the early morning, Troop Officers were sent up to recce their positions. Full of enthusiasm they arrived in Breskens just in time to see the P.Ws. from the fort go by—it had just surrendered of its own volition. Faced with 2000 uncartoned rounds for return the RASC were not amused. And for three days Speedy was simply unbearable. As for the subs—bastards—led by Cliff Shone they'd polished off the last of the whisky.

On the 24th 10 Troop with a half troop of AVREs under Captain Bailey moved to Ijzendike with a view to assisting in clearing up Oostberge. In Oostberge itself the acting C.O. of the Queens Own Rifles of Canada explained to Captain Bailey that the town had been cleared as far as the end house of the row which straggled out on the road to Zuidzand, but that the whole thing was now held up by a position round the small pit some 200 yards ahead. The leading platoon reported profuse mines in depth on the surface of the road but might be able to lift them during the night. Anti-tank guns not known, no cover and flanks and front wide open. And just what did he propose to do about that ? Orthodoxy in these conditions did not apply. Nothing could be gained by a large party—one 88 could wipe off the lot. So it was arranged for an AVRE lieutenant to lead and petard the bunkers, close on his tail a Croc (Sgt May) to flame, which could turn in the entry to the pit, and behind that Captain Bailey just to stooge along to earn his pay and give support. At first light you could see this trio with the big Canadian platoon commander in the lead jumping rapidly from house to house, through windows and doors to beat a sniper to the draw to the O.P.—the lavatory window of the last house and very convenient too. Some of the mines had been removed from the road but the verges looked suspicious. Terry had brought the whole party into Oostberge down a road still under fire in order to make sure of getting there on time and arrived split minutes before zero. The party immediately set off, passed the platoon position and the AVRE blew its left track on a mine. But he was in petard range and fired the old dustbin. Sgt May pulled over his to right and started to flame. Captain Bailey got to the second word of "Don't pass that tank" and never finished it—said "Blast" instead. Sgt May, always keen and willing to take a chance, had drawn alongside and hit two teller mines which broke two tracks and smashed several bogies. However the guns were still going and a small group of dejected prisoners came out whilst the Canadians walked into the position without casualties. Most of the Germans had left the night before, presumably in search of liquor in the cafes up the road. Stroud put in a neat single shot from his Besa and clean as a whistle downed a German running down the road, obviously thinking he was late for opening time. Distant German reaction on the left then set in, 75 HE hitting the houses. As HE has a nasty habit of turning into AP and the party was now a sitting target with no further function Captain Bailey baled out the crews of AVRE and Croc until things quietened down. Later that morning in spite of snipers and HE the AVRE chaps recovered the AVRE and very creditably shifted the mines. Sgt May spent an uncomfortable night in his Croc being continuously shelled, a direct hit smashing further bogies.

On the night of the 26th the remainder of the Crocs still "on the road" arrived in Oostberge—giving a total party of about 9 unhealthy Crocs and 3 HQ tanks—and in order to avoid shelling the Squadron now had its first experience of the troglodyte existence which was to characterise all campaigns in the next year. Amazing how the cellar of a shelled house can be transformed into a palace with the aid of a few mattresses and a "kackel" —can't do a thing without a "kackel," must have it. A troop of Flails and some more AVREs came down too, quite a nice party.

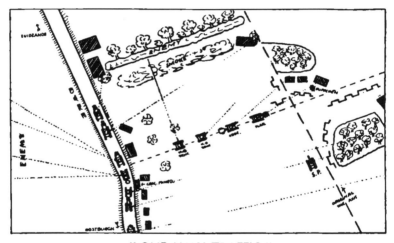

" ONE WAY TRAFFIC "

The advance was still held up—this time by a company position on the right. Turn right off the Zuidzand road by the aforementioned pit at 032122 and there is a small track running some 1000 yards to a cross tracks. And just beyond the cross tracks on the right is an orchard and farm—this the Germans held and all attempts by the company of Queen's Own on the right to get at them or past them had resulted in dozens of casualties from MG fire and anti-personnel mines.   An S.P. which had tried to come up the same axis had brewed-up on mines and the "funnies" were now asked to devise if possible an attack from the main road, Captain Bailey being given a troop of flails, some AVREs and as many Crocs as he wanted. Pass to you.   Again it was an unorthodox situation and an interesting little problem of simple mathematics.   The track was metalled and flails soon wear out flailing continuously on a metalled road.   On the other hand it was no good waiting till a tank went up because the ground on either side was impassable.   It was decided to sacrifice the wear and tear of one Flail.   Moreover advancing down this track meant crossing the entire front of the enemy, who had good positions in a long hedgerow and line of trees.   Large parties again were out—if the Flail stopped, the Croc would never turn round.   It was therefore decided that the artillery concentrate on smoking off the enemy front, the Flail should flail as far as the position, covered by all the tank fire it was possible to muster, and Terry Conway with his Croc then follow up with the infantry and flame, given close support by Captain Bailey.

At 1545 hours on the 27th the smoke was going pretty well and the Flails, Crocs and AVREs were firing everything they had in alloted arcs covering nearly three quarters of a circle.   The Flail set off and after 100 yards received a direct 75mm hit on the jib, rendering it useless —it made a tricky turn-round and came back.   Another one was launched, slowly flailing its lonely way down the track and the supporting tanks keeping it up for all they were worth.   As the Flail approached the cross tracks Terry Conway and Captain Bailey set off as hard as they could with the infantry to catch him up.   Bonko also set off down but after a short distance a large size HE on his engine deck smashed the engine and brought him to a standstill.   However that didn't stop him carrying on with a perfect shoot.   Simultaneously with Captain Bailey he saw a group of Germans dash into a barn just NW of the cross tracks and within split seconds 95s from Shave and Rispin were pouring into it, burning the whole place down.   Once over the cross-tracks Terry started to

73

flame and the Germans started to come out. Captain Bailey concentrated on sweeping the area on the left from which fire had forced the infantry into the ditch near the cross tracks. They carried on up the ditch however to their original objective and collected the Germans as they came out, some 73 P.Ws. The minor position on the left turned out to be a clever collection of slits dug under haycocks on sticks and in a hedgerow round a farm. It was just beyond flame range but was so shot up that it is doubtful whether they would have shown much more fight. However the infantry declined an offer to shoot them in and said if the flame couldn't reach they were quite satisfied to consolidate where they were for the night in the farm on the right. Thank you—good night. Terry had turned round in the farm and was now coming back followed by the Flail then this got ditched.

It was getting dusk and the artillery smoke had ceased, the tanks substituting instead. Most of the HE had been used. Captain Bailey pulled left at the cross tracks, whilst Terry crossed over, and then backed on to the Flail, Terry using up all his local smoke round the two tanks until they were hitched up. The procession set off back until stopped by Bonko's tank, still waiting for an AVRE to reverse down the track and pull him back. A 20mm was firing direct from somewhere in the line of trees and all four Besas were kept firing incessantly up and down the hedgerows until the AVRE arrived. It was dark by now but the whole area was lit by houses and farms blazing away—it had been one of the most destructive tank shoots ever. There was a spontaneous postscript to this in the Ecu d'Or in Ghent some days later from a Canadian Officer—"Gees, you don't know how many lives you saved that day". By next morning the whole thing had loosened up, the Germans, as was subsequently found, pulling back. The advance was ready to recommence.

It had been decided that a company of the Queen's Own would push on to the cross-dykes at Oostbergschebrug, supported by a half troop of AVREs and 9 Troop of the Crocs, whence another battalion should be launched on Zuidzand with fire support from more Crocs and AVREs under Nigel. Accordingly at 0800 hrs on the 28th supported by Peter from the pit firing on all likely OPs Captain Bailey bowled along with an AVRE and the leading platoon. It was suggested that every house be petarded but suspecting that the birds had flown Captain Bailey confined the fire to scattered Besa, much to his relief later as the white-faced terrified Dutch occupants emerged. The start line for the new phase was thus secured with no further misadventure than a wounded cow and three sleeping German soldiers kicked out of their hiding places and loaded on his tank. Profit— one fine diesel truck. One of the prisoners had a very fine service watch. On their return, before the crew could even get their earphones off, Nigel had duly whipped it. Stroud and Underwood never forgave Captain Bailey that—nor ever will if they ever get to know that it now resides on Dicky's wrist.

Nigel's party now rattled up to the start line. George Storrer went on ahead and past the start line, where to his astonishment he saw the Queen's Own platoon walking unperturbed, intent on taking Zuidzand on their own and blithely oblivious to the fact that hefty Canadian artillery was coming down there any minute now, sort of thing. George got caught in that artillery and says its a darn sight more unpleasant than the German stuff. However thus warned the platoon got away with it. Zuidzand itself was taken with scarcely any opposition and the whole menagerie was returned to Oostberge, there to make merry on Peter's welcome find of a Black Market stock of liquor and be joined by the majority of the echelon.

On the 29th the tanks moved to Retranchement with a view to supporting the North Novas in Knocke, already half taken. All spare crews were sent up to help the Canadians march back the amazing column of some 3000 P.Ws. that now came down the road. It was a most motley crowd—old men, young men, Mongols, Russians, Germans, Poles, French, the long and the short and the tall. And amongst them only one God's gift to humanity—a ravishing girl in riding breeches and white blouse, flowing hair and proud face, who walked along with all the poise of a great actress. Yes, mighty cute.

In the middle of the night Nigel took a select party in a jeep through the silent, deserted questionableness of the extensive suburbs into the fashionable resort of Knocke, and finally ran Lt.-Col. Forbes to earth in a large hotel in the town square. As the situation ahead in the mined and fortified area of Heyst was still vague no plan could be made, but it was agreed to bring the Crocs into Knocke first thing next morning. Accordingly at first light they crossed over the Canel de Derivation into Belgium over a *20 ton* Bailey and installed themselves in Knocke. Later that morning, cheered on by two lovely bits of stuff from a bedroom window, an imperious procession of HQ tanks, 6 Troop under Cliff, a troop of flails, and some AVREs began to shoot up the fortifications in Heyst, then move forward to blaze the trail for the infantry. As nothing seemed to be happening Nigel, George and Harry Bailey dismounted, walked through the heavy gate, booted out a few straggling Germans and penetrated to the inner sanctum. But Peter was already there, swigging a bottle of cognac and waving a Luger. "Too late old boy I got 'em all. Just sent the commandant out to you —didn't you see him?" In another room an officer stood up on his unwounded leg as Nigel entered and saluted. "You have fought well" said Nigel. "But you have fought better, mein Herr," gallantly replied the other.

And that was the end of the Scheldt party, except for a pleasant day spent in that very pleasant resort of Knocke as free guests of a populace mad with the joy of liberation— and of course bringing out the odd hidden bottle you know. Then over roads a foot deep in water, through the ravaged and desolate country to the more pleasant beds and confines of Sysele to await the move order for the long expected overhaul in Antwerp. Only two HQ tanks and eleven Crocs now remained. Sgt Brandi in a tortoise effort to meet a transporter had been indecorously bulldozed into a watery ditch to make way for the artillery going up on the Flushing show—and for all we know or care it is still there. Sgt May's tank had been recovered back to workshops. Still the echelon was now reaching something like a practical establishment with trucks and motor cycles taken out from Knocke. A party in Bruges, then visits to Ghent. Just the job. Finally on the 5th November the Playboys set off for the Eldorado, pausing one night near Ghent to take a last advantage of that lovely town.

J'ATTENDRAI

"Ah mon petit majeur ! Et monsieur le capitaine ! Oh là, là ! Madame, viens vite." And with this delightful feminine shriek the beautifully groomed and fragrant blonde scatters her American admirers to the four corners of the chic Embassy and throws herself around the fortunate recipients of those voluptious lips. Belgium has such a lot to give the world in that grossly under-rated art of kissing. Charming Madame, courteous and elegant, emerges in her fine black dress, more sedate in movement but with her eyes elated—and she restrains herself to the gentle but exquisite art of kissing on the cheek. This scene takes place some three months later when two officers are passing through—and it explains a lot.

Ask anyone in 'B' Squadron what they consider was their toughest battle. And they will tell you Antwerp. Ask them which is the finest city in the World—Paris, Brussels, London, New York. And they will tell you Antwerp. The city that was to change two songs, "J'ai deux amours, mon pays et Anvers" and "Oh ! Lord you made the nights too short".

But it is a campaign which to our everlasting regret and the world's loss must for many reasons remain a closed book. A gay kaleidoscope of wine, women and song played to the lilting melody of "J'attendrai". Punctuated all to frequently with the phut-phut of the flying bombs and the double-crack of the V2. And it may not be recorded. This is real tragedy indeed. For who if not the great lovers and the great topers are the real heroes of this world. Who more worthy to be sung. But the shadow of matrimony lies sometimes before and sometimes behind. And therefore hélas !

The "Playboys" were ensconced for the most part in Broechem with a short period in Merxem as and when their new Crocs became ready to take over. Goodly bases, both, from which to launch the Antwerp prowl. Broechem became one's continental home. Here in this pleasant village most everyone had a comfortable billet, often a bed, often too some fair maiden in the house—Sgt Brandi married one. And in the evening some twenty cafes from which to choose, each with its presiding queen. The sisters Julie and Jose—they too take their place in these annals. Vivacious Julie was past master in the art of raising expectation in the manly breast. And expectation was precisely where it ended. Though it is said of a certain officer who shall be nameless that she so far lost herself as to whisperingly invite him to spend a week-end with her in a certain pleasure spot in Antwerp. And to his everlasting shame he turned it down.

Staples, Hudson, Cheesman, Peck, painting Antwerp red. Dancing at the Flora. Partaking more than somewhat of that variable commodity, love, at the Splendide when funds were high and at the Liberty when funds were low. The Sardine Tin. Peck's pet "scrubber" was a blonde called Blanche. Mind you he'd had a little too much cognac or she'd never have pulled that fast one like she did. It was in the Cafe Kleineveste and they did a strip-tease all the way. Except that *she* at the final fling kept her bathing panties on. There was a dame who wanted Mills to desert, bags of money for both of them— but then Mills always did like the Army far too much.

The recce business was a somewhat costly one, but once you knew the ropes it wasn't all that bad.

Mike had come back from England. Lieut Bob Albany, pocket dictator, had turned up—you never saw the colour blue until you saw Bob's eyes after three tots of gin. Lt. John Tilley came in too—he didn't drink himself but he would ply you with the stuff.

Main basis of the evening for the officers was the Club where for one brief half hour of crowded glory you got whiskey at five francs a glass. It meant working pretty fast. Form was to split up over the adjacent tables served by three different waiters, all heavily bribed, and buy full rounds simultaneously at each. In this way you could down about twenty before the half hour was up—then go out to the Embassy and just keep topped up at fifty francs a time. You never had to worry because in some incredible manner at the vital moment Jones, the Major's batman, would loom out of the darkness of Antwerp wherever you were and look after you. Or it would be Elworthy, taking charge of the party in some slick dive and running the whole show. It was not beyond him to hide in a cupboard when the party were turned out and let them all in again. The "Duffel bags". Taking over any and every band, with the Doc giving drum solos to applauding audiences. "Quite alright really gentlemen. My real job, drummer. Medicine ? Just a hobby". George Storrer climbing lamp posts and singing bawdy songs. He escorted a nurse back to the hospital one night and she was out after time. So they decided to take a chance and go through a ground floor window. But it turned out to be a bedroom and as George's great body eased itself through the window the light switched on—and there all nicely tucked in bed was a girl who'd been to school with him. That was just before he left again for 'A'. Over Nigel's activities we draw a veil—the seventh.

You could even have fun shopping. Now "The—Boy" swears it was innocent necessity and maybe he was right. Anyway he'd got his eye on some of that nifty intimate apparel for his wife. But he didn't know the size—or so he said. So he put his arm round the fetching attendant, simulated for a few moments a faraway look and said "No, bit too large". So they brought another and the process was repeated. "No, bit too small". Well it was rather like a choosy dame trying on hats. In the end he'd tried out every pretty girl in the shop before he turned back to the first and said that maybe after all she was just about the same size.

It was very pleasant too to see Colonel Roscoe Reid again and have him come over for a visit.

But at last it was all over. Mike resumed command of 6 Troop, Cliff took over 9 Troop and Peter took over Recce Officer, a job which he was to perform extremely well. Tony Ward reorganised 8 Troop under Sgt Bullard. The new Crocs had been "shot in" and flame tested, done their road trials, the old HQ tanks had got new guts and took on a further lease of life. Everybody was flat broke anyway. On the 4th December the Squadron was moving east via Brussels to the mining town of Waterscheide, just NE of Hasselt, and entering on a further phase.

79

JUST GETTING AROUND

Looking at the big picture the first great surge was over and a static period now followed before the great final momentum was got under way.

In moving to Waterscheide the Squadron had again billeted itself on families, and once more we pay tribute to the great Belgian hospitality extended to both officers and men. It had also rejoined the regiment after a complete isolation of three months. That it was in 30 Corps Concentration area for a move east of the River Maas on Operation "Shears" was not unduly worrying. It's usual secret and reliable source of inside dope had it that, although the Squadron would move over the river and do a lot of play-acting planning, in actual fact no fight would take place and the Crocs would return to Holland within days—this in fact is what transpired.

On the 9th of December the Squadron moved over to Maastricht Bridge to Nieuwenhagen, almost on the German frontier. They were to support 214 Brigade to capture Hoven, Krandorf, Nirm and Blauenstein on the right of 43 Division advance. Cloth models, rehearsals, recces and the whole bag of tricks went on with little excitement around. It was quite obvious anyway to anyone who went and looked that tanks would never make the boggy ground, much less Crocs. Peter went on a forward recce in a wood, set off a flare and brought a hail of mortars buzzing round his head. Nigel and Harry Bailey removed their berets and crawled into no Man's Land, whispered sceptically to each other that they didn't think there were any Germans in the place, but crept back with undiminished care. One pitch black night they decided on a short cut through almost neutral ground visited by German fighting patrols. But after three miles map reading was impossible, so after a short discussion on the ghoulish events reputed to the area discretion proved the better part of valour and that jeep sped back with a speed not usually accredited to normal channels. A playful sortie to 'C' Squadron Mess was frowned upon. And on the 16th the operation was cancelled, the Squadron moving via Waterscheide to Berjeik, a little

80

Dutch village S.W. of Eindhoven.

Berjeik was noted for three things—its intolerable dullness, the charm of its nuns and Peter's astuteness. On arrival there two sick worthies of the Squadron, Cpl Russell and Hitchman, were quartered in the nunnery and had the merriest time of all. There were five of them, and Sister Charles was just about the most charming and inviting creature that ever sought protection in the veil. Well Cpl Russell and Hitchman were soon the adopted "brothers" of the sisters, and "sons" of the Mother Superior—and nothing was too good for them. Now Hitchman goes for the dogs and he'd soon got the whole fraternity absorbed in pictures of his dogs and greyhounds racing. Next he taught them cards—and religiously took their money off them every night. Cliff Shone just couldn't resist the place and was always in to see his patients. Whilst Captain Bailey was very partial to a spot of lunch there on his recces.

The Mess was in the house of the Catholic Priest and one night Peter, in a fit of jubilation, threw his pistol in the wash basin, thereby "accidentally" knocking a great big hole through it. Now in the cold light of the morning after this promised to be more embarrassing than it had appeared the night before. But Peter solved it neatly. He took Confession with the Priest—and the Father's lips were thus sealed on the matter forever more.

Short work was made of the month's whisky ration and then the Germans stepped in, breaking into the Ardennes and spoiling all the Xmas preparations. Monty started balancing his forces, which for 'B' Squadron meant moving on the 23rd to the cold Belgian barracks of Hasselt in support of 43 Div. On the next morning a very fine fire display was staged for the C.O. The Crocs were parked around the square and in the front of one a fire had been lit. From another behind there suddenly came a wet shot, going over the one in front and on to the fire. The fuel was ignited and the flame travelled back along the rod to the gun, setting the intermediate tank and trailer on fire.

Everybody was on to it in a flash however and the tank was saved undamaged, though not the trailer.

81

The "young man" had jumped into the blazing tank and driven it off. As he jumped out he saw the C.O., came up, saluted smartly—"Time you had an officer's type badge, Ward".

Orders had been received that Xmas day would not be celebrated with any undue consumption of liquor. How- Cpl Gough and his cooks set to and in some way best known to them produced a most sumptious repast. Moreover Peter returned from visiting Corps and Div and reported them in a complete and very proper state of intoxication and demanding why the hell 'B' Squadron wasn't. Followed by a personal L.O. from General Thomas to the effect that Christmas **would** be celebrated. So the beer went round and the buckshee rum, most of the chaps from somewhere produced a bottle of cognac. Salt was soon giving voice to sentimental songs, amazing how these tough guys go in for them, Cpl. Briggs "sending" Cockney songs. Nigel giving out the Ball of Kerrymuir to loud prolonged applause. Long after dusk the unmelodious vocal chords of Staples rose above the silence of Hasselt in the approximate strain of "J'attendrai". Nigel and his henchmen, reverting to type, were taking over the microphone at the local Café.

On the next day the Squadron moved to a little village near Bilsen. The roads were now inches thick in ice and when attemps were made to move out for rehearsals with the infantry the drivers couldn't do a thing, so the attempt had to be abandoned. However Monty's "balancing" was apparently already having a very sound effect so on the 31st of December the Crocs were sent back to Berjeik and the nuns.

Here on the 2nd January 1945 Lt. General Simpson, commanding 9 U.S. Army, accompanied by Lt. General Hobart, at a ceremonial regimental parade presented seven of the American decorations for the fine work done at Brest. From "Life" the Playboys were now breaking into elite society. There was a photo of the parade in Sphere and "London Illustrated"; and there you can see Nigel flanked by the "young man", looking very forthright, and Bonko looking more "Beast of Belson" than ever. L/C Harris, Tpr Clare, Tpr Lynn and Tpr Parry. And behind them you can see Peter and Cliff Shone.

"LITTLE WHITE FROCKS ON THEIR DARLING
LITTLE TURRETS"

REQUIESCAT

It was pretty cold these days, alternately snowing and freezing, and not at all a pleasant prospect for the impending operation with 52 Div. On 11th January our preliminary move order had come in and Nigel was attending a conference on "Blackcock" with 156 Brigade. "Blackcock" was a vital operation east of Maas to clear as far as the River Roer, preparatory to the Americans using it later as a jumping off ground in the drive west of the Rhine to meet the British coming from the north through Cleve. This ground was the German outpost area of the Siegfried Line and as such was defended with consummate skill and tenacity, in particular from tanks, S.Ps., mortar and artillery fire. It was to be the first time 'B' Squadron fought on German soil—and the desolation of the villages was now as wine to the soul. An interlude of bitter fighting in the most appalling conditions of ice and snow this operation will stand out always for the Playboys as one of uncanny good fortune and unqualified success. A success due in large measure to the dash, endurance and common sense of Nigel's personal leadership in contravention of all orders that he should fight the Squadron's battles from the remoter comfort and reality of a half-track.

On the 12th January tanks and Echelon moved up and arrived late next night in the new area, a small Dutch hamlet by the name of Klein Genhout just east of Beek. Conferences, lectures and demonstrations were the order of the day with the 5th H.L.I. and the 6th and 7th Cameronians. Nigel also contacted the Sherwood Rangers of the 8th Armoured Brigade with whom the Squadron were to work most of this operation—and let it be said here that the support they gave throughout was magnificient. 52 Div. were originally to take the centre, flanked by 7th Armoured on the left and by 43 Div. on the right. As the original plan went straight-way for a ball of chalk there is little point in giving it, the whole operation descending rapidly into a piecemeal grabbing of villages.

For the first day of the operation the allocation was 9 Troop and Capt. Moss to 5th H.L.I., 6 and 7 Troops under Nigel to 6th Cameronians and 8 Troop to 7th Cameronians for support on Havert, Linge, Stein and Hongen.

On the 16th the Squadron moved off to its assembly area at Lizenbroek just south of Sittard. Here the Crocs were tricked out in their cute snow camouflage, whitewash on the hull and little frocks from parachutes draped round the darling little turrets. It makes such a difference. Now they looked really chic and distingué—stood out a mile my dear on that dreary black and grey snow landscape. Simultaneously ducky little snowsuits appeared from nowhere for the officers—just when in order to avoid confusion with the Germans the infantry had decided not to wear them, had orders in fact to shoot anything in white whatsoever. Nigel rather fancied himself in his and was a bit peeved because it was wiser not to wear it.

The 7th Armoured had kicked off on the 16th and were rapidly meeting snags. D day for 52 Div was on the 18th and Roy moved off before first light, dropping 9 Troop half way between Sittard and Tuddern whilst he himself went up to watch the armoured group bridging effort commanded by the C.O. over the little stream at Linde. Nigel brought 6 and 7 Troops up to Tuddern, a little village just inside Germany, passing the elfin—like Cliff sheepishly divesting himself of his snowsuit. Here 'A' Squadron of the Sherwood Rangers were waiting to go through. Some fifty yards from their head solitary shells were landing time after time on exactly the same spot of a poor little cabbage patch, the safest thing out to watch. And here who should appear but Geoffrey Walker straight out from instructing at Sandhurst. "Damned extraordinary these "O" Groups out here—not a bit like we had them at Sandhurst, Nigel."

Unfortunately so far as tanks went the bridging effort was a failure and 'B' Squadron's A.R.V. spent most of that evening and the next day doing a very creditable recovery of bogged flails, AVRE's, and Shermans. Sgt Potts and Tpr Wear were in fact in great prominence throughout the whole show, not a day passing without them going up and recovering some unfortunate.

Linde, Stein and Heilder were taken by the 5th R.S.F.

alone, a V.C. being won on that day, and in Havert the 5th H.L.I. encountered little opposition. During the night the infantry went on into Hongen. Shortly before dusk the Squadron moved back down the road again into a little Dutch hamlet. Billets and hospitality were rapidly forthcoming and the Squadron got down to its last comfortable night for nine days.

Early next morning the infantry captured Saeffelen and a message came through asking for one troop of Crocs to support the 6th Cameronians into Breberen. Nigel wisely took two troops instead—8 and 9 with Roy Moss as well. Information about the enemy was most indefinite other than that Breberen was held. The ground was open and covered in snow, both flanks were wide open. Supporting the 6th Cameronians was also a Squadron of S.R.Y.

The roads were covered in ice, so that by the time the Crocs and tanks had skidded and slithered to Saeffelen very little time was left for planning and tying up. The infantry were advancing two companies up, 'B' on the right to take Breberen itself and the houses to the east, 'D' on the left to take Nachbarheid. Tony's troop with a troop of Shermans was to support the right. The distance to the objectives was about a mile and the Crocs were to advance as gun tanks until about 300 yards from the village, then go ahead of the infantry and flame the outer edges.

This recce group had assembled in full view at the road junction at 758723 just N.E. of Saeffelen—which asked for it and got it. A colossal mortar stonk came down, wounding several, amongst whom were the infantry C.O. and Cliff's company commander. With about two minutes to go to the 25 pounder concentration Cliff thus found himself amongst a bevy of subalterns with no plan yet made and debating as to which one should take over the company. Cliff became fatherly. "Look here, I'm going to flame the western edge and the southern approach, then you go in, I'll meet you in there and see if there's any more trouble". And off they went.

The Shermans stood off and blazed away at both villages whilst 8 and 9 Troops lumbered off over the snow, firing as they went. On the right Cliff's show went with

87

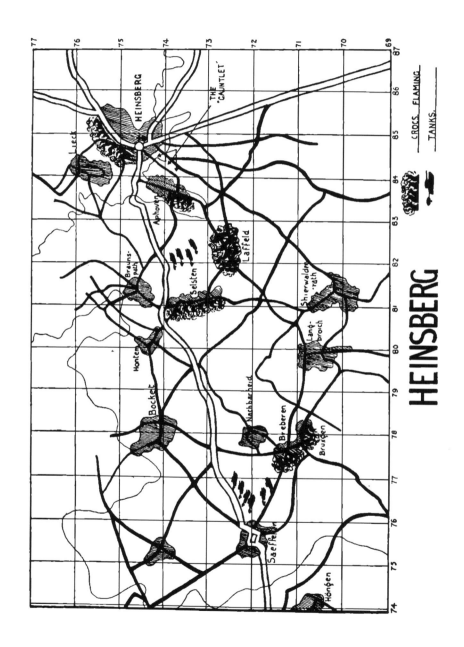

HEINSBERG

a bang. Terry Conway was a Croc commander that day and went in with Sgt Decent, burning and smashing the houses on the west. Cliff shot in Sgt Huxtable as he made a tidy mess at the southern end—then dismounted in all the confusion of flame and smoke to sort out the position. Prisoners were coming out now and Jerry was pouring mortars and shells into the place and all round it. Cliff ran the platoon commander to earth and agreed to lead the platoon up the street in his own Croc, flaming all the way. And so he did for about 300 yards until he reached a road block. Fortunately there was a turning left here and after another tête-à-tête with the platoon commander Cliff cut off here to go round the village and come in again from the north. In doing so Cliff met up with another platoon commanded by a corporal going in the same way. He dismounted again and took the corporal down to the village square, where a runner contacted him and asked for help on the houses to the east. By now the whole village was on fire and the troop had used up all its fuel but still had plenty of ammunition left. Cliff therefore ran back through the burning village to his tank just in time to see a mortar kill five and smash up four more of the infantry clustered round it. It took quite a time getting them from under the tracks. The crew bandaged them up with all their shell dressings and put them into a nearby house. Just then Nigel came up and Cliff ran over to give him the dope. He was stood just by the horn of Standard when some particularly vicious brand of high velocity H.E. cracked in and hit the pannier door, caving it right in and sending Cliff for a six in a cloud of smoke. Cliff picked himself up with a face as black as a nigger minstrel and got on with the job of giving fire support on the houses to the N.E. until the whole place was cleared.

8 Troop did not flame. Tony moved off to the appointed place for picking up the company commander and started to shoot up Breberen and Nachbarheid. The company commander however was killed and in the resultant confusion the company went in successfully with fire support alone from Tony.

The party sat in the open until late evening, being heavily shelled and mortared, shooting up the whole countryside until their release back to Tuddern. Here crews and fitters worked until the early hours of the morning, replenishing and getting the Crocs fit again before tucking themselves into the cold wet debris of the cellars to a brief rest. Meantime way back at Heilder Sgt Bullard's crew, their tank had broken down, were collecting eleven prisoners of war, ten of whom had bazookas.

By first light the whole Squadron was again on the move to an area east of Heilder, standing by at call. No use was made of them that day but at dusk the Squadron was split to very little purpose—unless there is a specific job or the front is very extensive anticipatory allocation very seldom pays, in fact quite the reverse. It wears the chaps out doing extra guards, strains communications to the limit and worst of all often means troops standing idle while the others are grossly overworked. Nigel took 8 and 9 Troops to the western edge of Saeffelen and somehow squeezed into the ruins. A sufficiency of "Kackels" being raked up the party suffered nothing worse that night than heavy mortaring. With 6 and 7 Troops Captain Bailey and Roy moved to Koningsbosch under 155 Brigade, establishing themselves in an outpost position. Their arrival was greeted with some surprise. "Damn glad to have you of course but really can't think of anything for you . Sorry". Koningsbosch was being shelled pretty frequently and the deep cellars were very welcome. But Roy's genuis for improvisation so excelled itself in the fixing of a stove that the officers were driven into the open, coughing and choking and cursing. Roy just dotes on kackels.

Next morning further splitting. 8 Troop came under the command of 156 Brigade. Roy was recalled from Koningsbosch and took 9 Troop under the command of 157 Brigade to Nachbarheid with a view to support on Hontem. Nigel took Tony to the Brigade conference, where 8 Troop were attached to 7th Cameronians for support on Selsten and Nigel immediately took steps to secure the release of 9 Troop for additional support. Fortunately he managed to see Cliff and give him some idea of the rough outline plan in case he was successful. This was to be Cliff's only directive.

The battalion recce party again met at a cross roads at 795735—and again bought it. Mortars came crashing

90

down on the enormous collection of vehicles and both
Nigel and Tony were only saved by an interposing carrier
—as it was both were wounded, Tony somewhat badly in
the hand. However he insisted on carrying on. The
plan was to get a firm ·footing in the northern end of the
long straggling village and then work south.

The attack was due to go in at 1500 hrs. and with only
a few minutes to go Roy's party got released, Hontem
having fallen. Cliff pressured up and bowled up to the
FUP at the cross roads at 795735 where the attacking
force were just moving off. Tony's troop was making
heavy going on the left. Cliff rapidly sized up the situation, picked out what he saw was the leading company on
the right, put his foot hard down on the better ground to
the right and got ahead of them, taking his troop into a very
pretty piece of flaming all along the western edge at the
northern end. Tony was unable to keep up at sufficient
speed but was giving fire support. The Sherwoods with
great dash came on all the way. As the infantry went
in for· the kill Cliff stood off to guard against a reported
armoured counter-attack coming from the S.E. whilst the
Shermans went on to have a look-see. Nigel now sent
Tony's troop up to take Cliff's position, and Cliff with Sgt
Huxtable and Sgt Decent (Terry had lost a track) started
to go down the main street flaming away with 'A' company.
In this way they supported the infantry for about a mile
right on to the final objective. Tony meanwhile from
outside the village was banging in H.E. and Besa ahead of
the infantry for all he was worth on a pre-arranged system
of Verey lights to indicate their position. Not until
nightfall did Nigel bring the Crocs back to Saeffelen.

Meanwhile in Koningsbosch Capt. Bailey's party
was changing hands with bewildering rapidity and no
material change—the various units under whose command
they came had not even jobs for themselves.

On the next day, the 22nd, Nigel succeeded in getting
6 Troop into play and Mike came up from Koningsbosch
to go in on Laffeld, leaving behind· his share in the whisky
bottle—no, not at all damn generous of him, just forgetful.

There is an elaborate trench system running the whole
length of the village just west of Selsten, then bearing east
at its southern end towards Laffeld. The assaulting forces

91

—5th H.L.I., 'A' Squadron of the Sherwood Rangers and 6 Troop—were to form up in these trenches in the lee of Selsten. From the bend onwards 6 Troop were to lead with a troop of Shermans and flame with one company from the church east, whilst the others cleared the north and west. Tanks and S.Ps. were to put down as much smoke as possible on the south, still in Germans hands.

Again the party was hurried. Roy and Mike arrived in heavy shell fire a mere five minutes before zero and by sheer good luck dropped into the same trench as the company commander. The party moved off in a hail of shelling and mortaring, the infantry getting some protection from the trenches. Sgt Wetherell hit a mine and brewed up, the crew bailing out without casualty. Mike went on with Sgt Hewitt and the Shermans. He waited a bit at the bend for the infantry, who did not turn up, so went straight on, covering Sgt Hewitt while he flamed the allotted span and more. Here the infantry came and went in, Mike going up the village and checking they were happy. He must have been under observation the whole time because wherever he went stonks followed like his shadow, most embarrassing when you're on an icy road and it's taking you about fifteen minutes to make a single turn.

Mike stooged around for the rest of the day until released, well and truly ditching himself on the way back. There was a photo in the Press of Sgt Wetherell baling out with a caption "moving hurriedly away with important equipment." Most definitely—the tank cooker.

Tony left for England on a hygienic course, the delectable fruits of which were borne in that exquisite "Ladies" in the woods at Weeze. Terry took over 8 Troop as Schondorf came into the picture. Here the situation was confused. Nothing had been heard of a company of the 7th Cameronians who had entered the village on the afternoon of the 22nd. A company of Glasgow Highlanders set out at about 0130 hrs that night to relieve them and had been forcibly prevented by heavy fire from the southern end. At 0200 hrs Nigel, Peter and Terry were called to a conference with the object of relieving the beleaguered Cameronians now believed in enemy hands. An attack was laid on for first light with

IN GERMAN MINEFIELD

War on the West Front has its penalties for both sides. Germans' minefields still hold perils for our tanks, but prisoners point back to our ropes.

This British tank is a German town on the Roer front, capture of right moving hurriedly away with while and except five during important equipment, bent too far the advance on Homburg, German which was commenced last night. Two of the crew can be seen on avoid a possible explosion.

one company of the 4th R.S.F., 8 Troop and a troop S.R.Y. Crocs and tanks at 0830 hrs first threw a smoke screen down between Schondorf and Hontem to cover the infantry over the open ground, then piled H.E. and Besa into the place. Still firing Terry now moved forward to lead the infantry in. But the 75mm salvoes had done the trick—about 50 prisoners ran out and the surrounded company was relieved.

That same day, the 23rd, Cliff was due to distinguish himself again—this time at Aphoven. At the last minute Nigel had managed to extricate 7 Troop from its fatuously negative role, too late to use them in the original flaming plan but very useful at supporting and reserve.

The Start Line for Aphoven was Laffeld. From here Cliff would lead the infantry, 5th H.L.I., with two Crocs on either side of the road and flame them into a firm base at the entrance to Aphoven, Cliff then pulling out to let the Shermans go straight through the mile long village with the same company to the other end without clearing up. Other companies would subsequently mop up. 7 Troop with the H.Q. Tanks and some flails were to sit on the high ground just west of the church in Aphoven, shooting up the village ahead of the infantry, putting a smoke screen down in front of Heinsberg and in general to shoot up everything and everywhere. Captain Bailey arrived from Koningsbosch just in time to see the column moving off from Saeffelen and, knowing nothing of the plans or situation, just tagged along to have a "shoot."

Cpl Phillips had spent the whole night fixing the one and only pair of snow-tracks issued and was not quite ready as the party moved off. So at the duly appointed 1300 hrs Cliff Shone cracked out of Laffeld followed only by those two old faithfuls, Sgt Decent and Sgt Huxtable. But he found it impossible to get off the road. Slipping and sliding he led his troop and the infantry straight down it. The infantry were being murdered by mortars as Cliff flamed and blazed away, getting them into the first bit of the village. He couldn't see any place for the Shermans to pass as planned so just carried on up the long street, flaming and shooting and shepherding his little flock of infantry along. One of the spandaus he saw too late. Just as its chattering flash from a shop window caught his eye his Croc overshot the mark. But in seconds he had Sgt Decent on to it—Tpr Hartland had it taped and just engulfed the shop and all the guys inside with roaring flame. After about 500 yards the road broadened and Cliff now pulled in to let the Shermans by. Turned round—no Shermans. The infantry went on whilst he waited but soon stopped, held up by machine guns around the next bend. Cliff gave up hope of the Shermans and decided to settle the matter himself. All hell was dropping on the village and as he crooned down the mike "O.K. Snash, advance" a large portion of it landed on the engine decks, blowing off the petrol caps and brewing-up the tank. Some of it went off in a diversionary raid to the back of Cliff's head and did it a power of no good. Cliff baled out his crew and collected them in a cellar, then went and saw Sgt Decent, telling him to pass his own Croc and do the necessary. As Sgt Decent moved off however he got in one hell of a tangle with a telegraph pole and its attendant cables—his hair got redder and his cursing got hotter but it was no good. There was nothing for it but to get down to a long job with a hefty pair of wirecutters. Nor on this ice could Sgt Huxtable get his great lumbering Croc past Sgt Decent. Cliff was now in a dilemma. If he kept his crew in the cellar the next company would be clearing and probably send down a grenade for them to share amongst them, if he kept them on the stairs they'd be shot at sight and if he kept them in the street they'd probably take a packet from mortars. But Sgt Decent's immobility and the infantry's plight decided the issue. Leaving Staples and Snashall in Sgt Decent's tank he ran and ducked with Fisher and Hudson right through the blazing village to find the Shermans. He found them still at the entrance, told the troop commander the whole position. Then relaxed into a R.A.P. from where he was evacuated to hospital. This was the end of "Blackcock" for Cliff. And not before time. He well deserved the M.C. that he got.

Meanwhile fun and games were in store for the supporting crowd, duly deployed from Laffeld and now sitting way up on the ridge to the west. From here they were knocking hell out of everything—mercilessly stonking the far end of Aphoven, putting down an extensive smoke screen, taking pot shots at the church in Heinsberg and all round it. A certain amount of H.E. and spandau was coming back, but as yet nothing to worry about. Nigel felt a hell of a crack on his head, giving him a large-size headache—there was a hole bored clean through his beret and a strip of hair and skin torn off his scalp. He put on his tin hat. Cpl Phillips had now joined up and took up a position on the right. This had been going on for quite a time and the battle just reaching its climax when the worst possible thing that could happen did happen— the commander of the show, Nigel, in spite of all protests was called out of battle for an immediate conference. Without the foggiest idea of what it was all about Capt. Bailey had to take over.

Nigel and Peter went off in Capt. Bailey's tank while the latter made a somewhat unceremonious dive through the cupola of Standard as a drove of bullets winged over the turret with the sound of a flight of geese. "Know anything about this battle, Mulvaney?" "Not much sir". "That's fine—I don't know that". "Cigarette sir?" from Bateman. "Yeah, last target?" "Major said not to fire anymore on the village as the infantry are up there." "Right just fill that smoke in a bit then have a crack at the church." "That do you sir?" "That's fine." Well whatever the situation was Capt Bailey did not like it, more especially looked at in reverse. The party had been sat still on that skyline now for too long and something pretty hefty should be along any minute now. Harry Barrow reported their smoke finished and the screen was thinning out. Ammunition was getting low. So Capt Bailey wired over for the Crocs to move back off the crest a bit, and as they started their cumbersome manoeuvres it happened. Next instant he saw Cpl Phillips brewing up, heard three solid shots in quick succession whizz over the top, saw all the kit disappear from Sgt Maddock's tank as an H.E. landed on it, saw a large piece of Sgt Brandi's trailer disappear and A.Ps. kicking up the ground all over with bags of H.E. making up full measure. In a flash the Shermans were scuttling back off the ridge in their beautiful reverse gear, not before a Flail had brewed. But it's no good trying to reverse a Churchill or a Croc and some had to lumber forward over

97

the forward slope before, hotly pursued by solid shot, they could turn round to "Follow me." Of course the I-C. failed at the critical moment and in answer to "Driver Right" Capt Bailey's tank turned three full circles, with Sgt Norrington in Peter's tank obediently conforming, before he got the party out. Harry Barrow tucked the Crocs in at the corner of Laffeld whilst the H.Q. tanks took up expectant reverse slope positions. An air O.P. who saw the whole party said that the fire had come from 5 Tigers and 7 S.Ps. which had sallied out from Heinsberg behind the smoke and taken up position to the north of Aphoven. Now there was the party in the village to weigh up. Altercations on the air produced the information that there were two Croc commanders in there, it might be Admiral Jones and Cpl Goon for all I know thought Capt Bailey, a little mobile at last and ready to rally back. With strict injunctions to avoid the skyline they hobbled slowly back into the fold. Tpr Mills and L/Cpl Allen now appeared on foot and gave the story of Cpl Phillip's tank.

After a wicked looking spurt in front of the tank and a hit in the engine Cpl Phillips traveresd the turret to put down smoke but it was too late. An 88 went straight through the turret, set off the ammunition and brewed up the tank. Tpr Brooks baled out of the pannier door, L/Cpl Allen stayed behind just long enough to retrieve 200 Weights and followed suit. Tpr Emm leaped out of the turret hatch, dropped head first on the ground and discovered he'd got two broken legs, about a dozen pieces in his arms and the same number in his back. Cpl Phillips came out with a badly wounded foot and Mills charged up after him with a piece in the leg. Matters weren't improved by mortars coming down all round. Tpr Brooks, a fine soldier if ever there was one, picked up Tpr Emm on his back and started off for cover in the nearest houses. Allen and Mills helped Cpl Phillips along. Tpr Emm was singing "Donkey Serenade "for all he was worth and cheering on his mount. Mortars and bullets were flying all over but somehow they missed them, and as the slow procession reached the fringe of houses some infantry stretcher bearers dashed out and took the whole party to a R.A.P. From there it transpired Brooks ferreted out an infantry commander amongst the ruins, pinpointed on the map and then on the ground the exact spot of the A.Tk. gun and in general supervised its destruction by an S.P. Then went over to the burning Croc to see if he could recover the flame gun, but the flame had already reached it. He received the M.M.

This was the whole party accounted for and just then Nigel's voice came up over the air ordering the party to return to Laffeld and prepare for a night march and action at first light. Tank state of the party now pretty grim. Two Crocs brewed. Sgt Maddock with a shot through the hull which had bust up the side welding so that you could see daylight, smashing a bogey assembly and starting a great oil leak in the engine. Sgt Brandi with a large chunk out of his trailer, Sgt Decent with two days work required on his tank. Still nobody was grumbling— none but the Playboys could have sheer luck like that and come off so light in men.

Back in Laffeld the fitters, the crews and echelon went to work whilst Nigel outlined the plan of operations in the town of Heinsberg to the commanders. During that night the 7/9 K.O.S.B. were to proceed under cover of darkness with a battery of S.P. 17 pdrs. and make a firm base in the area of the cross roads at 848746, just inside the town where the big building stands. The S.P.s were to encircle the town and ring it off from tank counter-attack. During darkness, when this was complete, one armoured column was to proceed to the firm base and assist the infantry clear the eastern edge at first light. A second column would then go down after first light and assist in clearing up the eastern edge, going down under cover of artillery and tank smoke. The route lay down a track starting at 835738, in full view to the enemy from front and both flanks for nearly a mile from the bend to the town. By darkness and smoke it was hoped to outwit the German anti-tank guns and S.Ps. The first column was to consist of 8 Troop and a troop of S.R.Y., with Peter and Captain Bailey. The second column under Nigel consisted of three Crocs from 7 Troop and Sgt Huxtable, a troop of S.R.Y., himself and Roy Moss.

As soon as they were ready the Crocs set off on the long slow procession through the night to the F.U.P., lined up along the street in the southern edge of Aphoven. Not until 0630 hours was the first column ordered down and first light was now perilously near with the going as it was. One Croc had already been lost in a ditch on the way up. The tanks slipped madly all over the road as they moved off and Captain Bailey's slid straight into a ditch. He sent Terry on whilst changing over to Peter's tank, Peter remaining as operator. "Haven't worked a wireless in years, old boy. Do you mind?" "Not a bit." Next snag came at the turn-off for the long run down the track to Heinsberg when Sgt May's tank couldn't make the turn and got well and truly ditched. Sgt May and Tpr Smith were wounded by mortars as they tried to get it out. Terry proceeded on alone, taking full advantage of darkness. By the time the rest of the party (Sgt Bullard, Captain Bailey and 2 Shermans) had circumvented Sgt May it was breaking daylight, and there was no steerage on Captain Bailey's tank because of a telegraph pole dragging on cables wound tight round the idlers and final drive. The light was still bad however so he sent them on and got down to it with a pair of wirecutters. Sgt Bullard and the first Sherman made it O.K. but the second one bought it from an anti-tank gun from the right on the last lap. As Captain Bailey and Peter jumped back in their tank this was the cheering news that greeted them. It was now broad daylight and artillery smoke as planned for such a contingency was asked for—but the artillery was otherwise engaged. The S.R.Y. Squadron commander said he would try to get down a little smoke and the tank set off round the bend on its lone run through the gauntlet. It was Hodgson who got it through by superb driving. The tank smoke had not built up and was in the wrong place anyway. Peter got the smoke mortar jammed after two rounds—cigarette drooping typically from his lips he was cursing and making cracks as he tugged away. "Just keep that foot hard down Hodgson," from Captain Bailey. But Hodgson was driving that Churchill like a Sherman— down the slope flat out, swerve hard left past the knocked out Sherman on the fields, bucketing over the ditches and banks with the shots kicking up spurts behind, onto the road and into the cover of Heinsberg. The fastest Churchill miler ever.

The infantry C.O. had his headquarters in the big building at the cross-roads, which was already receiving the attention it invited. There was a deserted air about the ruins of the town. The C.O. estimated, most incorrectly as it transpired, that only some ten Gemans remained and therefore had changed his plans with a view to getting cracking straight away. It was therefore agreed to allot the one and only Sherman with Terry Conway to the company clearing up the west side, Captain Bailey and the other Croc to the company clearing up the east.

At this moment against the instructions of the infantry C.O., who said that he did not require further armoured support, the second armoured column was ordered down. The smoke was still not very successful and two Shermans brewed up on the way down from anti-tank guns on the north. Just before turning on to the road into Heinsberg Cpl Jenkins ditched his Croc. Covered by smoke from the remaining Shermans and their own 95s Roy and Nigel did their damnedest to pull it out under murderous mortar fire, but all their efforts were in vain and it subsequently took four direct hits. This gave another Croc in reserve for each party but for the time being they remained in the area of the cross-roads. Heinsberg was now an isolated little island, surrounded on three sides by the enemy and the fourth completely covered by them. Nothing could get in and nothing could get out.

The infantry had not seen flame in action, so before starting up the main street Terry gave a demonstration shot to his company with entirely unsuspected consequences —from the houses all round emerged some fifty Germans. This cheered up the infantry no end. Terry supported 'C' Company throughout the day, flaming as required over very difficult going and the tricky business, not always possible, of avoiding observation from S.Ps. and Tigers which swarmed outside. The infantry C.O. was loud in his praise of this Croc. Not a single casualty was sustained by the infantry from small arms fire though many Germans were rooted out. At about 1400 hrs Terry ran out of fuel and Roy brought up Sgt Huxtable to carry on the good work until the whole of 'C' Company's area was clear. Roy too had some pretty sticky moments getting round the icy corners under direct fire.

On the eastern part the company wanted first of all to clear the perimeter which was impassable to tanks. However Captain Bailey suggested fire from the cross-roads and brassed up the first few houses before the infantry went in, then dismounted with Peter to watch their progress from the ruins of a shop. You could see there were no Germans in this part but the infantry were being murdered by the shells that now came down thick and heavy on the town. Shells literally poured into the place, heavy stuff and high velocity from all directions. The big building seemed to be the favourite target and they were hitting it almost every time. Yesterday it was Cpl Mulvaney cracking at the church, to-day Schmidt was having a crack instead.

There is a high wall extending from the building and the shop is just opposite. One must have hit the top of this wall because Peter had just made some extravagant crack when he dropped down and rolled over, losing consciousness almost straight away. The shells were raining down but Hardy Norrington who was stood beside them ran over for a stretcher, then pulled the tank up to the shop front for protection. They took him to the R.A.P. down in the basement where Nigel assisted the Doc, cool as ice though three times shells hit the building just above the basement window and filled the place with blast and smoke and flying fragments. But it was no good—in fifteen minutes Peter had died.

The stonking was tremendous. Hour after hour it went on never ceasing, wounding chaps, killing chaps, sending others "bomb happy". Fortunately the infantry C.O. was really tough. Bang, bang, bang—every few seconds—Jerry was down to it in real earnest. The wounded, impossible to evacuate them, lay in the basement all that day. A Tiger nosed up to the perimeter and one of the concealed S.Ps. brewed it up. It was now almost certain death to walk around on the cross-roads and the crews, even Davenport, stayed in the Crocs closed down and positioned against counter-attacks. "Hardy" was doing operator now to Captain Bailey. "Sad day, sir" and proceeded to cut slices of bread and jam, then produced some self-heating soup. Steady as a rock,

Norrington. He won his M.M. many times over in action.

The remains of the company clearing the east now came back, ready for the next bit. Captain Bailey accompanied them up the main street until stopped about three quarters of the way up by a large bomb crater across the whole street, but there was no longer any sign of Germans. By late afternoon the town was declared clear and the Crocs were released. Not that it made much difference. There was still no way of getting out—the only thing to do was wait till dark, listen to the shells and watch through the periscope the bits of shrapnel sizzle on the turret. It was clear that a large proportion of them had been sent forward without any real information as to whether they were necessary or not, and were consequently subjected both to direct tank and anti-tank gun fire and extremely heavy and accurate shelling without the majority being required. Only Playboys luck had helped them out again.

Round about 1830 hrs Nigel led the whole party out of town in the moonlight. Even so, as they roared up the slope fixed line firing had a few final pots which missed. Bonko, now carrying Harry Barrow, had stopped by Cpl Jenkin's Croc to pick up the flame gun and immediately got showers of mortars down. Setting off again his engine stalled and the battery was flat. Followed a period slightly tense in the deserted spot whilst the charger chugged away—Roy sometimes your language is most unpardonable.

Sgt. Norrington and Captain Bailey strolled back down the hill to investigate the wireless silence and a most heated argument started as to whether you could or could not start up with the auxillary charger going. Underwood lost that one. But finally they were all back in Aphoven, safely heading back in little groups on the long treacherous journey back to Saeffelen, there to do maintenance until the early hours. 48 hours solid, most of it in action, without a moment's sleep.

On the way back Nigel met Mike, who had been ordered to an 'O' Group for an action in the morning, and went with him. Neither the infantry commander nor the S.R.Y. Squadron commander however had any job for the Crocs, had not in fact suspected that they had any, and thought that anyhow they'd had enough. So that Mike's fatuous little party of two Crocs churning over the snow from Saeffelen were turned back by Nigel and the whole party at last went to sleep.

Pretty badly battered in regard to Crocs the Squadron spent the next day in reorganising. In relation to Crocs brewed and hit and the number of fierce actions fought the casualties to personnel had been astonishingly light— one officer killed, three officers wounded, six ORs wounded. On the 26th they moved to Leijenbrock and on the 27th were once more on the way to Berjeik, "Blackcock" finished and done with.

The whole operation was probably Nigel's finest achievement and richly deserved the M.C. which he got.

Peter was buried in his beloved Bruges, attended on his last trip by Nigel, Harry Bailey, Cliff Shone and the remaining members of his old 9 Troop. For the officers and the whole Squadron it was a great personal loss. A loss for which words and phrases are completely futile so we just leave him there.

THE BATTLE OF THE RHINE.

Back in Bergeik for a brief respite the Playboys could once more get down to the serious things in life—one evening for example the month's whisky ration, another the remains of the cognac, But so brief. By the 1st of January Tempo with 8 Troop was already giving demonstrations in Tilburg to Scottish units of 44 Bde. Mike took 6 Troop over to Nunen for training with 53 Welch. By the 2nd of January Nigel and Harry Bailey were in possession of the outline plan for "Veritable."

Operation "Veritable" was the real battle of the Rhine, the real coup de grâce against an Army which had decided to fight it out with crack paratroops on this side rather than his own. For this reason, and because at the crucial moment the Germans flooded the Roer, the original plan did not go at all according to schedule. In principle, however, it remained basically the same— a British and Canadian break-through of the Siegfried Line northern extremities onwards as far as Cleve, swing south and clear everything between the Rhine and the Maas. Simultaneously the Americans were to sweep up north and join up. Flooding of course did not allow of the latter for many days, with the result that the British and Canadians once more drew upon themselves the weight of the defences and were committed to long and bitter fighting reminiscent of the bridgehead days. What had been considered as a campaign of several days lasted in fact over a month. During this period 'B' Squadron tagged along most of the time with the forward troops, unable however because of the floods and woodland to give much assistance until the last bitter days of the Xanten bridgehead. However for the moment all was optimism.

First round was to be on a five divisional front, 15 Scottish Div taking the centre with its right flank resting on the Reichswald and 53 Div. On the appointed day 46 Brigade were to capture Kranenburg and the Spur about 814548. During the night armoured columns of Flails, AVREs and tanks would then breach and bridge the Siegfried defences followed by 44 Bde in Kangaroos, the tanks of the Grenadier Guards, and 'B' Squadron Crocodiles for clearing up at first light. Through this firm base 227 Bde would then leap-frog on to the Materborn feature. For this phase a thousand guns, a million shells and a colossal air programme were all lined up.

The Crocs were sub-allotted beforehand to each battalion of 44 Bde. Nigel was taking 6 Troop with 5 R.S. and 3 Squadron Grenadier Guards for clearing the area east of Tuthees. Roy and 8 Troop were going in support of 6 K.O.S.Bs. and 2 Squadron Grenadier Guards. These would not cross the Siegfried until first light and unless required. With 7 and 9 Troops Capt Bailey and Douglas Peacock (now Recce Officer) were to go through the Siegfried that same night and on as far as the Hingstberg and Wolfsberg features as best they could for clearing up with 6 R.S.F. at first light.

By the 6th February the whole Squadron was assembled in its various groups in Nijmegen, setting off on the evening of the 8th to take their allotted place in the column for the approach march to the F.U.Ps. Owing to the appalling conditions of the flooded ground and road blockages the progress of the column was extremely slow. It was night now and raining steadily. Monty's moonlight cast its half light over the desolate landscape. All through the night the column crawled along and as day broke on the mud and rain it was still west of the Frasselt-Kranenburg line.

However, taking full advantage of the good progress of the leading troops and the tremendous effect of the guns, 46 Bde had been pushed on to take the objectives originally assigned to 44 Bde, which task they had accomplished at first light. During the late afternoon the column again got mobile. The armour headed over the rough tracks, passing the ominously bogged mass of 'C' Crocs up to their turrets, through the floods of Kranenburg, over the minefield, the anti-tank ditch, the trenches and bunkers of the improvised Siegfried extension to Nutterden. Roy's group was in the lead and he very shortly got himself a job. Leading elements were already beyond the dominating Materborn feature towards Cleve, but the situation was rapidly becoming fluid. Large parties of Germans were still left behind and reaction was setting in

106

from Cleve and S.E. of the Materborn.

Towards evening Roy was hurriedly called up to see a K.O.S.B. company commander who was stuck along the road leading to the look-out tower west of Cleve, with his leading platoon pinned behind the house at 877557. The company was under fire from all directions and more especially from the houses ahead and on the right running up towards the look-out tower. Roy found the company commander after some difficulty, ensconced in a Kangaroo in somebody's back garden and in the direct line of fire. Politely declining his invitation to chat perched on the outside of the Kangaroo, Roy enticed him to the more friendly shelter of the ground. When asked if he could fix the Jerries in the houses Roy said, "Sure thing, now what about some infantry to go in afterwards?" He was offered a section. Roy laughed this one off in usual Rabelaisian style, but the company commander then pointed out the trip wire encircling the offending houses on the right and straight ahead, which in all probability indicated mines. He had lost so many section commanders that day that he could not possibly risk another until the arrival of reinforcements. In the end Roy agreed to flame with the sole object of attempting to scare the Germans from their fire positions.

It was quite dusk as Terry's troop came up, with no time for lengthy orders, and owing to some confusion as to which were the houses it was necessary to flame Terry took over the lead.

It was a lovely sight as Terry's Crocs poured flame into every house in turn, twisting and manoeuvring to get through the trees. The houses burned like tinder and the Germans fled. From the low ground of Nutterden the rest of the Playboys were giving silent applause as they watched in sympathy the impressive party. Impressive too as a symbol, the first flame used beyond the Siegfried Line. Skylined on a hill in the dark, and seen at distance, a flame show is almost a nostalgic sight—the long feathers orange red soaring through the darkness, through the outlined trees and in the treetops. The fitful décor, seen in breathless detachment, of a fierce game of life and death played out in its own flame-lit arena.

In the course of their long perambulation one Croc

tore away the trip wire and churned around on the suspected ground. No mines went up and the company commander now changed his mind, sending in his boys with complete success. All firing stopped. There was nothing now but our own infantry walking in the flickering light cast by the blazing buildings and Roy brought the party down to Nutterden.

Here the whole Squadron gathered together in the cold wet ruins of the few houses and snatched a few hours sleep, undisturbed except for the intermittent shelling in the fields and back gardens of their homes. Bob had brought up the requisite portion of the echelon in spite of floods and chaotic congestion on the single road.

At first light Captain Bailey was out with Geoffrey Crowe, a most promising newcomer, and 9 Troop to a R.V. about a mile west of the look-out tower. Here an armoured column of a squadron of Scots Guards, Crocs, AVRES and flails were to form up, preparatory to moving into Cleve with 46 Brigade and clearing up the very confused situation now existing there. However owing to the fighting which now developed round the look-out tower, and the extraordinary MFU now developing in Cleve, the departure of the column never did take place. Later in the day in fact Captain Bailey was mildly astonished to see Nigel with Mike and 6 Troop hustling by at full speed in the wake of 13 Squadron Grenadier Guards, followed in minutes by Roy and Terry with 8 Troop going through the same meteoric performance with 2 Squadron. His reactions were only surpassed by his astonishment when, a few minutes later, he himself was caught up in the maelstrom, doing a mad "Tally Ho" towards an unknown objective on the tail of 1 Squadron, and ending up in darkness among the F.D.Ls. at the little hamlet of Brasserburg about a mile west of Cleve. Here paratroop fanatics had infiltrated up from the S.E. and were conducting themselves in a very obnoxious manner—it was therefore a very wet and cold night, spent in the tanks under very heavy and accurate mortar fire and the constant chatter of nearby spandaus. Roy meanwhile after a nebulous chuckha round had returned to Nutterden for the night, but Nigel was also uncomfortably tank-bound for the night at 863548.

At dawn Roy rejoined 2 Squadron Grenadier Guards at Brasserburg whilst Captain Bailey's party dashed cross-country with 1 Squadron to the hotel just at the bottom of the look-out tower hill where 6 R.S.F. were reported surrounded. Here however for the expenditure of two boxes of Besa two Guards Churchills rooted out some 30 Germans under a most fanatical officer, and the party now stood by to move into Cleve just down the road. For some mysterious reason next minute 2 Squadron were dashing through, and Roy suddenly found himself having a pretty hectic time of shelling in bomb-smashed Cleve. The great question in Cleve was now as to which Brigade was doing which and with what and to whom. In fact who held Cleve, British or German ? And it was a long time before it was finally agreed it must be British.

True to his reputation Bob brought up the petrol, rations and water to the look-out tower long before any other echelon got through and quite oblivious to the stonks that were now coming down on the tower hill. Before he departed this party, and later Roy's, were recalled to Nutter-den. Because of the appalling mud Bob, in his own inimitable way, cajoled the command tank to act as mother hen to these wheeled chicks. Time and time again the two HARs were pulled out of ditches and fields and each time as the command tank rumbled up there would be Bob, blue eyes blueer than ever through his glasses, "Look, won't take a minute." Then came the final glorious shambles. It was snowing hard now, pitch dark and the narrow winding road just a mud-track. The road at 848555 was complete chaos, utterly blocked by struggling vehicles and traffic completely stopped both ways. The HARs were now behind and as the tank turned off the road into the boggy orchard alongside they followed on by mistake in the dark and sank up to their axles. So both were now hitched on to Capt Bailey's tank in line ahead. At which precise moment the roar of an engine, the whizzing of tyres and the spray of mud alongside announced the simultaneous arrival and full stop of the worthy water men, Whittingham and Tuit. Bob again became eloquent. By dint of complicated manoevres in the trees, snow and pitch blackness they were finally hitched up on the rear HAR and now, line ahead in tow, under Dougie Peacock's expert eye this magnificent caravan wound and lurched its way through ditches, trees and farms to something approaching terra firma. Roy's party came in later just as cold and soaked.

A day then of relative peace and quiet, trying with no great success to get dry and watching the lazy air-bursts overhead.

On the evening of the 13th half the Squadron, 6 and 7 Troops, were put under command of 4 Tk. Coldstream Guards and moved into Cleve long after midnight to join 1 Squadron, preparatory to doing a hackneyed "in case" advance on Rosendaal, Moyland and the woods between. Owing to flooded roads the advance had ultimately to be made on the axis of the secondary road running through Bedburg. Rosendaal itself was quickly captured and whilst the Crocs took some shelter from the shelling in the lee of the houses between Bedburg and Rosendaal the command tank went off with the tanks, giving fire support to the infantry from the road. In the evening the half Squadron were released and the Crocs therefore took over the basements of the houses and began to transform them into homes. They wern't the quietest of billets—on the first moment of arrival a shell bounced inches away from the command tank and disposed of several infantry. This heavy shelling and mortaring continued for several days and had a nasty habit of bursting in the tops of the trees just across the road. Add to this the constant furore blazing back from the gun lines just behind—the wild pleasing echoes of Normandy gunfire. Everything else was fine and dandy—mattresses, tables, cutlery, crockery and delightful dishes of chicken, potatoes and other good grub found hoarded away. Pearson cooks a very pretty chicken and Mike was getting grossly overfed.

That same evening, the 14th, the half Squadron were ordered to report to 44 Brigade in Cleve at 1000 hrs. next morning. However such is the natural course of MFUs that at 0830 hrs next morning Captain Bailey was taking a gentle breather at the front door when 1 Squadron Coldstream Guards pulled up outside and demanded airily if the Crocs were ready to attack Moyland with them, H hour in five minutes or so. The Crocs stayed put whilst the command tank moved off to the cross-roads at

Rosendaal, knowing nothing of the plan but the final objective. The German stonks were coming down here in true British style—heavy concentrations repeated ad nauseam, and the infantry taking enormous casualties. Progress was therefore very slow and wasn't helped any by the tanks being road bound and capable of nothing but distant fire support. At 1200 hours over the air a message that the half Squadron should be with the Grenadier Guards and 44 Brigade, and not with the Coldstreams. Despairing of his sanity Capt Bailey pulled out and proceeded back to Cleve to sort out the situation. Here it was decided that the Squadron should remain with the Coldstreams, and Capt Bailey again dashed back to find Douglas already called out to the cross-roads with 7 Troop already pressured up. At this stage the Coldstream Guards Squadron was strung down the road to Moyland with about a mile to go. The right had not been cleared and on the left the leading platoon was just entering the farm buildings at 955528.. Though utterly useless because they could not get off the road the Crocs were now called forward to assist in the approaches to the line of wood just ahead running from 959524 to 958523. Before taking them down Captain Bailey went down instead, locating after some difficulty the leading Platoon Commander, whose patrols came back in a few minutes to report the strip not held and who therefore released the Crocs as he was consolidating for the night. On the way back the command tank blew up on a box mine, thus stranded as the leading representative of the British Army on that flank and most uncomfortably exposed to view in the gathering dusk. Douglas Peacock spent a very eerie night manning it with the crew and at first light in spite of extremely accurate and observed mortar fire recovered it with great élan, the crew taking two P.Ws. into the bargain.

On the 16th a plan was made for 1 Squadron Coldstream Guards and the Glasgow Highlanders, using Crocs, to attack Moyland this time from the south on the 17th. Basically the plan was for the Guards to sit on the high ground in the woods and shoot up Moyland whilst two flails and 6 Troop supported by the command tank were to be launched down the road that runs from 965513 to Moyland. At the same time Dougie Peacock was to

111

take 7 Troop down the road from Rosendaal and flame a company of 7 Seaforths into the buildings on the right at 962519—that same night however these buildings were occupied by Seaforth patrols.

On the 17th 6 Troop duly moved into a forward assembly area just short of the FUP but the attack was finally called off because the Start Line had not been secured. Next day Mike was lined up again in the same place, but once more and this time finally the attack was cancelled because the Glasgow Highlanders were being pulled out of the line. That same day the half Squadron came under the command of 2 Canadian Div.

Meanwhile the remainder of the Squadron under Nigel were making the best of the miserable lodgings in the ruins of Cleve, waiting for the armoured break-through of the 11th Armoured Div. Tony had come back to take over 8 Troop again, thus releasing Terry. Roy had gone on leave and Cliff took his place. For a few days, except for hectic planning of ops which did not transpire, the Bedburg boys were left in peace and quite. Nigel now hared off to the precincts of "Bobby's Bar". Michael went sick to hospital—bronchial catarrh he claimed but obviously a surfeit of chicken really—and John Tilley was suddenly given two minutes in which to get to India. 'A' Squadron therefore very kindly lent the Playboys two good types— Ron Corney and Rex Lowe, who were to be very valuable on the night of their arrival—Corney taking over 7 Troop and Rex taking the half-track and echelen. The ever smiling and adapable Terry came down, to take over 6 Troop this time.

On the afternoon of the 25th the half Squadron at Bedburg said goodbye to its billets and moved out as support to the South Saskatchewan Regiment with 'B' Squadron Sherbrooke Rangers on to the wood and high ground in 0084 and 0147 south-west of Calcar aiongside the railway. This was part of a much bigger plan in which 6 Canadian Brigade were to capture the high ground to the south on the right whilst 5 Canadian Brigade took the high ground south-west of Calcar, the attacks thus forming a base from which to launch the Armoured Divs. Further over on the right the British were carrying out a similar plan. The attack was to be a night drive on to the distant objectives with Shermans blazing the trail followed by the infantry in Kangaroos, which were to return under cover of darkness. It was quite obvious that the Crocs could not do a single thing as they were intended for precipitous bit of wood which dropped almost sheer down to the road beyond, that in fact daylight would find them all in their naked glory doing damn-all on top of an open hill and just dead meat for tanks and anti-tank guns miles around. Nevertheless needs must be when the unknowing drive and the Crocs took their place in the procession. At dusk the column moved off cross-country to the FAA some miles away. The ground was appalling and Crocs, Kangaroos and Shermans were bogging down right, left and centre. Only the two command tanks made it and these only just. These now retraced their tracks and sometimes singly, sometimes both together each using three tow ropes, worked away until five of the Crocs were successfully debogged, Dougie again being the calm maestro of recovery. At long last the party reached the FAA where the remainder of the column were snatching some sleep. Not so the Crocs. Tpr Brooks, of whom we have heard before, had taken off the inspection plate and was doing his damnedest to switch over a stuck petrol cock on to the full bank. When this failed he tried with a stirrup pump to transfer the petrol from the full bank to the empty one but to no account, whereupon the tank went back some way and scrounged every possible jerrican from an obliging battery commander, coming back just in time for the move-off. Already so heavy had been the going that every Croc had used up half its petrol, and still the same distance to go once the attack started. The start of the column was delayed and as there would now be no check in the F.U.P. the Crocs were pressured up.

At 0340 hrs, some twenty five minutes later, the column crashed into the F.U.Ps. and on to the Start Line. If anything the going now was even worse and only the two command tanks and two Crocs managed to cross over the Start Line.

The air and artillery programme had now reached its zenith. Ahead and away over on the right flash after flash in the sky denoted the bombs and the shells as the column forged towards them. Monty's moonlight now

113

revealed what is always one of the weirdest spectacles of war—a prepared night attack using armour cross-country. On the Start Line itself everything was chaos, the Germans staging here a beautifully timed counter-attack at the crucial moment. The stuff was coming down pretty heavy and didn't give much chance to collect thoughts and check. But the column pushed on regardless. The speedy Shermans and Kangaroos, if they didn't get bogged, were now whizzing along in the weird half-light, straight through to their objective, clearing nothing on the way and leaving the slow moving Crocs way behind. The whole area was now covered in shell and mortar bursts, the red Bofors directional shots lazed overhead on to the objective and kept you on the bearing, angry bursts of machine gun tracer were shooting around in every conceivable direction, and from the farms ahead and around bursts of tracer came flying straight at the turrets and somehow just zipped over the cupola flaps. Of the two remaining Crocs one now bogged itself and the other developed a leak, losing all its pressure almost immediately before getting bogged. The Kangaroos, having disgorged their infantry, and the two leading troops of Shermans loomed up and went by, belting back now hell for leather from the objective in an attempt to get off the dangerously exposed escarpment before daybreak. As dawn broke Ron Corney and Douglas Peacock were doing wonderful recovery work under constant and accurate small arms fire and mortar, the bullets pinging on the side of the tanks from about 100 yards away every time they exposed themselves to hook up a shackle. A burst of Schmeisser from a farmhouse some 70 yards away just missed Ron Corney but he jumped inside and had his Besa on it in no time. The command tanks were now getting dangerously low in petrol as orders came through to reassemble a little way back at 969488 and get fighting fit again. The command tanks emptied their tanks and tore the guts out of their engines as they laboured to pull out the Crocs, leaving only one up to its turret. For an attempt to achieve nothing an exhausting and creditable failure.

Here near the farm buildings the fitters got cracking straight away on the badly leaking Crocs and the ailments of the command tanks after their strenuous night and day, Cpl Allnutt taking time off only when some wicked 88 A.P. sniping shots came whizzing by at the party, which it was impossible to get under cover. Of the whole party only one Croc was fit. Another uncomfortable night under shell-fire was spent in the tanks and next day the the half Squadron were put at one hour's notice whilst Captain Bailey slipped off to Town for an R.V. with Nigel in "Bobby's Bar". That same day 8 and 9 Troops under Cliff Shone's command slipped out of Cleve, linked up with the 159 Brigade of the 11th Armoured, and moved forward to Halvenboom, some three miles from Udem. The Americans were now coming up fast with nothing to stop them and from the north, with many casualties but slowly and inexorably, the British and Canadians were squeezing the fanatic German paratroops into the bitter Xanten pocket.

On March 2nd Dougie Peacock with 6 and 7 Troops got down to a little interior economy, still at the farmhouse where the little party had rallied after the night attack. Baths for the men. Then the half-track acting as scavenger— to wit towing away 13 dead cows, 2 dead horses and one sheep. All love's labour lost. Roy Moss, returning from the uxorious happiness of England, without time to collect his kit was rushed into an 'O' Group with 214 Brigade and preparations went ahead for 6 and 7 Troops to move early next morning, when the half Squadron duly checked in at Kehrum. They were immediately required for an attack with 'D' Company of the 5th D.C.L.I. on a wood just north of the Hochwald Forest. A spectacular barrage came down behind which the Crocs and infantry moved up until the Crocs were brought to a full stop by an un-suspected anti-tank ditch on the edge of the objective. Much perturbed Dougie got out on foot and finally con-tacted dear old Major Lonsdale, already consolidated on the objective without a shot being fired on either side and full of invitations to dinner.

The Crocs returned to Kehrum where later Roy met a Canadian gunner demanding what the hell all the row had been in the wood that morning. Apparently he was innocently intent on fixing up a forward observation post in the wood when he'd been well and truly stonked by the

115

barrage, then turned round to find himself facing the insuperable odds of a half Squadron of Crocs and a whole company of infantry with fixed bayonets. Such is war—sometimes. Nothing more spectacular occurred during the day beyond being commissioned to tow away trees from the road beyond the F.D.L.S.—a job needless to say which the crews finally had to do by hand.

On the next day, the fourth, Roy was called to 214 Brigade with the object of supporting the 5th Worcs in an attack on Wardt, but careful recce showed the ground far too waterlogged and cratered to use Crocs. In actual fact the village was taken without a shot being fired. During the night however a patrol reported a crater and anti-tank ditch some 1000 yards ahead of our F.D.L.S. down the Xanten road which was held by the Germans, and in all seriousness the suggestion was made of a mischief raid by one platoon and one Croc on the ensuing night. Of such consequence sometimes are the lives of men. Fortunately the Brigade Commander was capable of envisaging the fruitless loss of life this would entail and at the last minute managed to get the enterprise cancelled. Not before Dougie Peacock and Terry Conway had carried out a very creditable if amusing recce. In order to see the crater it was necessary to crawl over a good stretch of No Man's Land to a windmill forward of the F.D.L.S. This they had accomplished in safety and were now peeping from behind a mound at the crater when, with a hell of a clatter and the banging of a door, the windmill disgorged two terrified German women all oblivious to the presence of Dougie and Terry. That is until the latter laughed—whereupon one jumped six feet in the air and shrieked to the high heavens. On being assured however that no shells were labelled for the "Windmill" they calmed down and, recovering from the shock of not being raped—perhaps a little disappointed in fact—they returned to the windmill's shelter.

At 1000 hrs on the 6th 214 Brigade informed Roy that he was required to support 129 Brigade, to whom he reported at 1500 hrs. The German Xanten bridgehead was reaching its last bitter spasm before the Germans, decisively beaten on the west of the Rhine where they had made a fatal decision to stand, were at last blotted out on

116

XANTEN

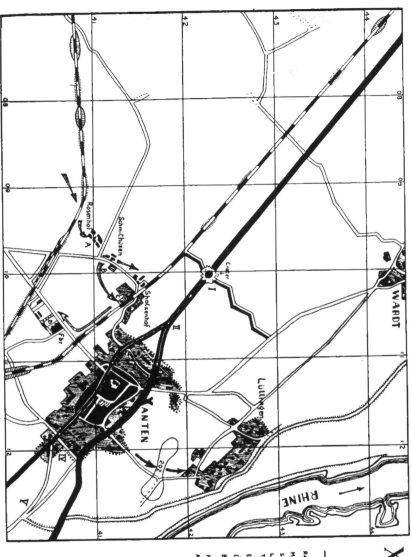

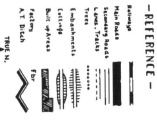

this their last foothold. The half Squadron were now required to support 4 Somerset L.I. in a two brigade attack on Xanten from which a Canadian Battalion had the night before taken a bloody nose—as we shall see the rest of the Palyboys were to be similarly engaged. But first of all Roy's party were to protect an AVRE bridge-laying party over the crater and anti-tank ditch which we have just mentioned. At 1300 hrs on the 7th the whole party moved up to Marienbaum and in the early evening firm orders were given out.

Xanten lay very much in the open at the end of the long dangerously straight road down which the attack was going. On each side of the road the ground was treacherous, and thickly scattered trenches made the water-logged terrain almost impassable to Crocs and tanks. The anti-tank ditch was rendered continuous across the road by the large crater, estimated at some 50—60 feet across, the road itself being lined by trees and built upon a bank about 10 feet high. Xanten had been bombed pretty heavily and gloomy prospects of cratering and debris raised their heads, though air photos seemed to show the road as passable. Remains of 1 Para Corps were holding the town, tough guys and in some strength. A Canadian battalion had already been sent packing in some confusion and S.P. guns were also reported in the offing. The Para boys too had excellent artillery support, both from behind Xanten and worse still from across the Rhine as well.

129 Brigade were taking the left of the attack with 4 Canadian Bde on the right. There was no supporting armour. Within 129 Brigade 5th Wilts were taking the left on to Luttingen, supported by a Squadron of heavy armoured cars which in actual fact were brought to a full stop almost at the start by cratering. 4th S.L.I. were taking the right, straight down the main road, trusting to the Crocs—relying on a Squadron of AVREs and a company of Engineers with a 70 feet skid Bailey bridge to get these across the crater. The ditch crossing party consisted of a platoon of infantry, one Crocodile command tank (Dougie), a troop of Crocs (Terry Conway with 6 Troop), an AVRE command tank, two fascine AVREs, a Churchill bridgelayer, four AVREs carrying the skid

Bailey and two Sherdozers in that order, designed to reach the crater at 0530 hrs. The infantry were to provide local protection and to clear the ditch and houses in its immediate vicinity whilst the Crocs acted as gun tanks and gave close support . The fascine AVREs. were to attempt to cross on the right of the road, the bridgelayer on the left. If these failed the Crocs were to hide up in a small farm on the right of the road whilst the Bailey was positioned. Failing this there would be no alternative but the bulldozers. From here the battle would enter Phase II, 'B' company pushing on with Dougie's Crocs to form a firm base at the forked road. In Phase III 'C' and 'A' companies, supported respectively by 6 and 7 Troops, would capture and clear the areas shown on the maps, axis being the main road. Whereupon 'D' and 'E' companies in Phase IV would pick up the Crocs and advance to the end of the town, thence exploiting in Phase V as far as the perimeter road. Throughout the battle the left flank was to be smoked off and two troops of S.P. Valentines were also to protect this flank from suitable positions.

At 2100 hrs that evening Dougie Peacock pulled out with 6 Troop and joined up with the AVREs. in an F.U.P. on the main road. Here they grabbed some sleep in the tanks. In the cold darkness of 0430 hrs Dougie with the Crocs was heading the whole cortege single file down the road towards the crater, arriving there dead on time at 0530 hrs as the thunderous creeping barrage opened up, and pulling off the road into fire positions as arranged to let the bridging party go through. The chatter of Spandaus and the crack of snipers from some 100 yards on the other side was the German reply, the infantry platoon being the chief attraction. But Dougie and Terry were already warming up the guns, brassing up everything the other side with a vengeance, and the Germans quietened down. The infantry took the ditch and the bridging operation commenced as the Croc party stepped up the guns. The ground on the right was very boggy and it was the Churchill bridgelayer on the left which first laid a very pretty bridge. Straightway Douglas and two of the Crocs were across and back in the road again—Sgt Wetherell bogged to such good tune that two AVREs. could not pull him out. 'B' company had just crossed over and were waiting for the Crocs, but it was some time before Douglas managed to run the company commander to earth in a house on the left. Dougie was brassing up the houses on either side of the road and each side was exchanging pleasantries as Tpr Brown calmly strolled up from Sgt Wetherell's tank and to Gledhill's disgust cooly whipped the front shackle. Sgt Norrington now decided to have a fling and was soon on foot vigorously chasing Germans back to the infantry who were quite a way behind the Crocs. Things were going smoothly now, the Crocs lumbering on ahead and plastering the houses with Besa and H.E. until the Germans came out. An anti-tank gun opened up from the left fork but was quickly hit by the leading Croc's 75mm. Tpr Hill in the command tank, in spite of a poisoned arm, followed suit in split seconds—a perfect bull. Round and round spun the anti-tank, gun for all the world like any roulette pointer, and a white flag came out. From the right hand fork heavy fire was coming from a mill but two 75s dead-on produced the white flag and the infantry walked in to fetch them out. 'B' Company were on their objective.

Meanwhile Roy, and 7 Troop commanded by Rex Lowe, had with difficulty crossed the ditch and now came up with 'C' and 'A' companies—Phase 111 was going in. On the left Dougie and Terry kept on moving up, blazing away, moving up. As each target was pointed out they lammed in the 75s and out came the Germans every time. Smooth, suave, deadly. In no time 'C' Company were on their objective and the prisoners going back. Roy and 7 Troop had shot 'A' Company over the 200 yards of open ground on the right and the party were approaching the town itself when the infantry were pinned hard down by heavy Spandau fire from the buildings ahead and on the right flank. Whilst Roy delivered his usual robust bashings on the right flank Rex, with Sgt Maddock, charged straight up the street and now for the first time let them have the flame—great belchings of it into the houses on both sides. Germans were soon cowering back to our lines, many prisoners being taken and 'A' Company carrying on now without further loss. At the Archways the Crocs were brought to a full stop but Roy in his command tank, blazing away, threaded a tortuous passage through until the third crater proved impassable—but this was 'A' Company's objective and they were now successfully on it. Phase IV going in. Dougie couldn't get through the craters on the left with 'E' Company so Roy ordered him back to the fork—fortunately this company met with no opposition and was soon on its objective. At this moment from out of the blue appeared a Canadian bulldozer. Though it had nothing to do with this operation Roy prevailed on it to fill up the craters and alone in his command tank was soon heading along with 'D' Company. He didn't spare the 95 and Besa and this not unnaturally had the desired effect on the houses, which rapidly disgorged their defenders until 'D' Company too were on their objective. So far so good. Altogether 150 fanatical prisoners besides the Germans killed, and our infantry casualties fairly light considering the fierce resistance. And that is why General Thomas personally congratulated Roy on the half Squadron's achievements that day.

On the left, however, things had gone pretty well astray. 5th Wilts, trying to take Luttingen from Wardt, had got a bloody nose and at 1630 hours urgent orders came from 129 Brigade to refill and refuel the Crocs for an evening attack from Xanten to Luttingen with 4th Wilts. The Div commander however decided that the Crocs had accomplished enough for one day and postponed the attack until 0630 next morning. Roy spent most of that night planning it. He sent his tank back to have a crack at towing out Sgt Wetherell but it only succeeded in bogging itself. So Sgt Wetherell parked himself for the night in the front room of a house nearby and on the next morning was mildly shocked to find a German soldier hiding in the cellar in a chest of draws—no he didn't leave him there.

"H" hour was finally fixed at 0715 hrs and next morning, the 9th, the Crocs were there, crossing over the Start Line with the infantry and heading steadily first of all for the kidney shaped hill just south of Luttingen, which was taken without opposition. The Rhine itself now only 400 yards away. Rex Lowe with 7 Troop then charged the village, pouring flame into the outskirts, and the

121

infantry went in without casualty, taking twenty one prisoners including an officer. Some Wilts prisoners taken in the unsuccessful attack the day before were also released.

Short of crossing the Rhine, which was considered a major operation, the Crocs could go no further—Roy therefore took the party back to Marienbaum where it came under command of 2 Canadian Div. An L.O. arriving in the early hours to say a rep was required at first light at 7 Canadian Brigade wasn't very welcome. This Brigade had the task of taking the railway bridge over the Rhine at Wesel with the Crocs in support. It was dependent however on 5 Brigade first taking Ginderich and at 1100 hrs the scheme was cancelled as the bridge had been blown. The great battle west of the Rhine was over and the German Army defeated. Planned to last a few days it was now a month since 6 and 7 Troops slipped out of Nymegen and during the whole of that time, fighting or not fighting, they had been in the thick of it and not once able to relax.

And what of Cliff—trust him to be getting into trouble. We left him with 8 and 9 Troops moving forward from Cleve towards Udem on the 28th. The next few days were spent in continuous changes of command and planning, and always moving forward. 2nd March Sgt Driver and Tpr Moore were wounded by shell-fire. On the 4th a plan was laid on with 4th Mons to clear the road south of Sonsbeck, but owing to the large number of troops converging 11 Armoured Div were withdrawn on the 6th and the plan cancelled, Cliff now coming under command of 2 Canadian Div in support of 4 Brigade. Whilst 129 Brigade attached Xanten from the north 4 Canadian Brigade were going in from the west, and from this flank too the Playboys were to show their metal. On the 7th they moved up into a forward position in a wood alongside the railway at 072408, about two miles west of Xanten. At 0530 hrs on the 8th, at the same time as Dougie was opening up in the crater with the Somersets, 4 Canadian Brigade also crossed their Start Line. three battalions up, to the thunder of artillery. The Playboys had not long to wait.

Cliff was with Brigade H.Q. as adviser. At 0930 hrs the call came over. The R.H.L.I. were held up by heavy fire from the houses in the area 096411 and it was up to Harry Barrow, now in a command tank. He went forward to an R.V. still, as it turned out, in enemy hands and contacted 'A' Company commander under heavy mortar and sniper fire. The Company commander was killed outright but Harry carried on planning with the next. In next to no time Tony's troop, supported by the blazing guns of 9 Troop, were sailing into the German houses (A) under cover of their own smoke and with flame belching forth. Tony's Croc bogged, but not before some fifty to sixty prisoners came tearing out and the R.H.L.I. went in. Geoff Crowe, who was to win the M.C. that day, now moved up closer and when a house at 097412 (B) gave trouble belted straight in without a plan and flamed out Germans into the waiting hands of 'C' Company Essex Scottish.

'B' Company next hit trouble in the shape of a strong-point some 600 yards ahead round a large house at 103414 (C). A plan was soon tied up, but when Tony tried to get down the road he ran into two large-sized craters. He cracked off with his troop round to the left but the ground was a morass and here again he couldn't make it. Meanwhile Geoff Crowe on foot had done a tricky job under heavy fire of recceing a route round on the right to take the place in the rear. The infantry now came back from the left and went in behind Geoff's troop as, supported by Harry Barrow and 8 Troop, they wallowed along the muddy ground and charged into the house with their flame guns full out. This difficult and creditable manoeuvre had the desired effect—over 80 prisoners in all came out.

At 1400 hrs 'A' Company were pinned down from the factory some 600 yards S.E. at 107407 (D). Harry Barrow fixed up to meet the infantry rep down the road but both this rep and his successor were killed by sniper fire. Small arms fire was now incessant and observed mortars were raining down in the area. Another R.V. was arranged a little further down the road but Harry Barrow's tank shed a track on the railway. The Crocs were trying to get up to the factory and the whole thing now resembled a slow horse-race with hazards, down the railway track then turn off right into the boggy ground near the factory. Sgt Huxtable's track was half off and he was crawling along in an effort to get it on. Sgt Decent bogged down seconds afterwards, and Tony Ward close behind did the same. This left of the whole party only Cpl Briggs still going strong—he had taken the left of the road but he too could now get no further and stood by to help in recovery or brass up the factory. Geoff Crowe's crew were soon out and hooking on shackles but the mortaring now became colossal. Within some 30 seconds about a dozen mortar bombs pitched on the turret of his Croc and only Snashall managed to get back inside unscathed. Geoff crawled back, dazed and wounded, to Sgt Huxtable's Croc, now halted. Sgt Huxtable's crew now showed what it was made of. Jack Huxtable with Bundock hared along through the bullets and mortar fire and finally reached Geoff Crowe's tank. There they found Tpr Uff dead, L/C Lewis dying and Tpr Molyneux lying alongside the tank very badly wounded. Whilst Bundock went back to a R.A.P. for a stretcher Sgt Huxtable dragged Molyneux back, though all hell was going on. As the two returned and reached their own tank another burst of mortars flung them flat on the face. Beach, Huxtable's gunner, now came out and with Huxtable—now running, now crawling—they got the stretcher to Lewis and carried him unconscious to Tony Ward's tank. But he died as they got there. Meanwhile Barnes, the driver, had climbed into Beach's seat and was giving the two covering smoke and brassing up the factory to hell. Somehow Huxtable and Beach got back—and took a long swig of rum. The only thing left was to shoot up the factory.

But this was to no avail and the situation as darkness fell was by no means pleasant. Sgt Huxtable's track was now completely off. But the infantry were first class, digging in all round them for protection, and in the morning, except for the odd rifleman who surrendered, the factory had been vacated. The area however still remained hot —shells and mortars came crumping down incessantly. Most of the Crocs were recovered next day, a very fine performance under heavy fire, but Sgt Huxtable's crew had to stick it out in their Croc for two days, being shelled and mortared the whole time.

At last the battle west of the Rhine was over. One by one the Playboys got together again.

CURTAIN

All Crocs and tanks in the Squadron that *could* rally did so now at Marienbaum on the 10th, from whence they moved into a regimental area between Weeze and Udem, a desolate forest area. It was some days however before the whole of them were in. Here, in the fortnight which elapsed whilst the preparations went ahead for crossing the Rhine, crews and fitters put in day after day working hard at the battered tanks and Crocs until they were once more fighting fit. There wasn't much fun around—west of the Rhine every village and town was nothing but a heap of dusty soul-destroying debris littered amongst craters. Still it wasn't too far to Nymegen, and the Sgts Messes had plenty of liquor waiting to be disposed of. A C.O's. inspection made a change. But, as Cpl Simpson will tell you, if only you have the sense to run the tank forward so that it tilts on the first bogey it's got to be a keen man who takes the trouble to climb aboard—and it isn't every officer who will approve of pipe racks fitted to the turret walls, or electric circuits designed to activate earsplitting sirens whenever the flame gun trigger is pressed. Anyway Bertie Mills didn't climb on a single Croc in 7 Troop.

Still the great thing in everybody's mind was "der Tag"—over the Rhine to the last battle, to "crack about" the German plains. And on the morning of the 24th in that melancholy forest of firs the C.O. was giving a well-timed lecture on the great operation. The night had been full of the roar of planes, the thunder of artillery and the crump of bombs. And now, as he finished, right overhead came the steady drone of the first wave of the great paratroop and glider armada—flying low and one of the most breathtaking sights of the whole war. Wave after wave to the grim, steady, relentless, vengeful, triumphant roar of the great engines. After the paratroops the gliders. Here and there one broke loose and the pilot would twist desperately this way and that to get free of the massed columns of planes. And sometimes one would disintegrate

125

in mid-air and drop like a plummet to the ground. As the first wave of paratroops topped the end of the forest and closed into dropping formation down there on the ground every Buff's heart went out to the guys up there. Flak was coming up now and in minutes the red devils were floating down into the battle of life and death. There was a solemn silence as the last wave went over. And then winging their way in their wake from out of the sky, flying in the most perfect and symbolic V formation, came a great flight of wild geese and disappeared into the heart of Germany.

The Playboys in the initial stages were in 30 Corps reserve—30 Corps were doing the left hand crossing—and alloted to 43 Div. In the early hours of the 27th the tanks and most of the 'B' vehicles left Weeze to the marshalling area S.W. of Calcar. At 1400 hrs 6 and 7 Troops with three Squadron HQ tanks left for this last great stepping stone—Roy staying behind with the remainder. At dusk the column had reached the Class 40 bridge at Rees. A few desultory shells were coming down and there was a long wait whilst the Engineers got the decision as to whether the heavy Crocs should be allowed to cross. Finally the O.K. was given and they trundled off one by one. Crossing the Rhine was definitely an occasion but commanders were so engrossed in directing the tanks, with inches to spare on either side, that there was no time to indulge in melodramatic cogitation. Through the still burning and deserted gaunt heap of stones that was Rees, and into harbour at 0230 hours in the morning in a field alongside the road to Millingen.

At 1100 hrs Nigel had orders to support 4th Somerset L.I. (129 Bde) in an attack on Dinxperlo, about three miles N.E. of Anolt, subject to Anholt itself being taken by 130 Brigade by 2000 hours that same evening. Everything was tied up and the tanks moved into an assembly area with the infantry at Bienen during that evening, ready to move off during the night and attack at first light. At 2100 hrs however the C.O. woke Nigel up to tell him that Anholt was still holding out and that he would be required to support 4th Dorsets to take it next morning, supported by 13/18 Hussars. Nigel and Dougie spent most of the night trying to find various headquarters in the pitch dark but finally had everything laid on—at 0600 hours the Crocs pulled out to a position about a mile N.W. of Anholt.

The plan was to attack Anholt from the N.W. and a bridge had been built over the canal during the night. The Crocs were to accompany various companies in the successive phases, Mike supporting 'B' and then 'C' whilst Harry Barrow took over 'A'. The route in was pretty exposed to anti-tank fire but smoke and speed got over that. 'B' Company, Dougie and Mike crossed the Start Line at 0930 and were quickly on their objective, a mere six prisoners being taken. The other companies were quickly on their objectives too, with no opposition—the Germans must have decamped during the night. No flame was required and at 1300 hrs the Crocs were released, but were not allowed to re-cross the bridge until 1700 hours. Some shelling was coming down and a Sherdozer brewed up from a mysterious shot that seemed to come from nowhere. Nothing more untoward happened and in the evening the Crocs moved back to harbour near the projected auto-bahn about two miles south of Anholt. At 1200 hours the half Squadron were released into Corps reserve and moved back. Anholt in fact, though it was not then realised, had been the last shot fired in anger by the Playboys on German soil. On April 1st the Playboys with 'C' Squadron moved back over the Rhine into the old harbour near Weeze and considered the war all over bar the shouting. A little peeved in fact that they would not be in on the mad rush through the liquor supplies. Only the echelon were employed—Roy taking off most of them on longer and longer journeys to assist the RASC in supplying the onward surging British Army.

On the 14th however it was discovered that the Crocs had not yet played their final hand and on that day the Playboys once more crossed the Rhine to Hockleton, bound for 1 Canadian Corps in Northern Holland. 1 Canadian Corps had just come from Italy and after the initial rush were beginning to find things a bit sticky. On the 15th through the pleasant, sunny, tulip-covered country-side the Crocs bowled along mile after mile way over to the little hamlet of Wilp, over the River Ijssel by ferry raft just S.W. of Deventer. It was good to be among a friendly popula-

127

tion again and in country relatively unscarred by the havoc of modern weapons. The Crocs had done about 150 miles on their own tracks in two days—good going.

Nigel was at 2 Canadian Div as adviser and on the 16th Captain Bailey with Terry Conway, and 6 and 7 Troops, were tied up with 3 Canadian Brigade. Roy with 8 and 9 Troops were tied up with 2 Canadian Brigade. The Canadians had reached the line of the canal and it was now planned for 2 Brigade to cross over at Appeldoorn itself and clear the northern half of the town. 3 Brigade were to clear the southern half. Roy's party were to support the bridging operation. Tony in his recce had cautiously reached the canal side and was looking at the occupied factory on the other side when the Typhoons gave him the shock of his life by tearing hell out of it. Captain Bailey's party in the initial stages were to do an indirect shoot. This however was later cancelled—rather fortunately as the requisite white tape had all been used up at Weeze, loaned to HQ, to make the place look smarter ! 3 Brigade in fact had a new plan, conveyed to the Croc party as it arrived in its new harbour for the night just east of Appeldoorn. A bridgehead had been won some miles south over the canal at 840950, a bridge was to be built during the night and then 3 Brigade would clear up the whole area from here to Appeldoorn and the southern half of Appeldoorn as originally planned.

No sooner then had the Crocs got out their bivouacs for the night than they were taking them off again and moving some ten miles throuth the darkness and over the the bridge at dawn, lying up just west of the canal. Capt Bailey went ahead and joined the battalion commander. The Germans had left about an hour before and the advance now became something of a triumphant procession, the great Churchill lumbering along with the infantry C.Os. jeep mile after mile to the cheers of the assembled half-starved villagers. They had nothing left to them but flowers and these they gave in thousands. The command tank in fact was given an imperial ovation and was soon for all the world like an exhibit from Covent Garden. Fresh tracks of a German tank were on the ground—it was about an hour ahead of us—and Mills was doing his nut because he had to stay on the gun and could not respond to the plaudits of the wenches. And so into Appeldoorn without a shot being fired—that is to say except for a crusty old Quisling who later fire a shot at Harry Barrow from an antique fowling piece and missed.

Roy's experience had ·been similar. Through the town sitting tailwise on his scout car and grandiosely taking the cheers and laughter. And when it was all over Glasscock said, "Your—— is showing". Roy felt at his trousers and there was a great hole through his shirt and various portions of his anatomy were flapping in the breeze. "Why the ——hell didn't you tell me before ?" "Well sir, as you were having the glory I thought you might as well have some of the humiliation too."

Canadian Div now decided to cash in and drive hard towards Amersfoort and Utrecht, taking in some twenty miles that day. The Crocs were now called up and every possible vehicle used to mount the infantry, the Crocs in each column taking a whole company on board. Captain Bailey was heading through the side-roads to Barneveld, Roy taking the main road on the north via Voorthuizen At 1400 hrs the motley columns set out. 3 Brigade were going ahead slowly but with very little opposition and halfway there, on orders from Nigel, the Crocs dropped ·their infantry and returned to Beekbergen for an evening's relaxation amongst the Dutch. Mills of course had to get mixed up in the wrong company, a religious thanksgiving party, and to his horror was asked to sing a hymn— however he obliged with some bawdy song, and as none of them knew English sufficiently well it was enthusiasti- cally acclaimed as a sign of real fervour.

To Roy however fell the distinction of the Playboys' last action, and a damned good one it was to be. About ten miles outside Appeldoorn, and about a mile east of the Remount Barracks of Neu Milligen, Roy was bowling along in his scout car with the leading troop of Sherman when an anti-tank gun opened up straight along the forest lined road. The Shermans manoeuvred off the road and proceeded to hot it up, but before they succeeded in giving it the K.O. Roy had quiet a hectic time pinned between two fires—he baled out of the scout car and watched the duel from a ditch. It now became apparent that here was a strongpoint, entrenched in the woods on either side, and the infantry were pinned. So Roy called up the Crocs and laid on a battle. As all the commotion was going on up came a jeep with a couple of inebriated Commando officers on board, demanding "Whish way to Amshterdam?" Roy said he didn't recommend it but they remained insistent until some really heavy stuff landed behind the hedgerow, knocking out quite a few of the infantry—in split seconds that jeep was a mere speck heading back for Appeldoorn.

Rex and Tony only had two Crocs each and it was decided that they go in simultaneously, taking left and right of the road respectively. Sgt Jackman led on the left, Jack Huxtable on the right. The woods were just right to burn like hell and they did. The Crocs went in with a tremendous concentration of flame and kept right on for a thousand yards until there was a great corridor of black smoke and orange flame. Tony was firing his 75 so fast that it sounded like a machine gun. The infantry company, of the Hastings Regiment, were magnificent and kept right behind, thus taking no casualties. Sgt Jackman's trailer was burning but Roy couldn't get him on the air so he blithely carried on. Right up to the road block near the cross-roads at Neu Milligen. Tony tried to shoot it down but the great wooden trunks just splintered. However a very heavy concentration from the Germans on to the cross-roads indicated that they had left, and the infantry now went undisturbed into the village. The result of this party was twenty-five terrified and dazed prisoners and a litter of horribly burned bodies in the woods—the Canadians estimated a hundred killed—and the Brigadier sent a personel tribute to the Crocs. It had been an excellent finale for the Playboys.

Roy spent a pleasant night in the lovely town of Appeldoorn and on the morrow the whole squadron concentrated in the little hamlet of Kootwykerbroek. But the advance had stopped. Ahead the Germans had flooded vast areas and Queen Wilhelmina, believing in the imminent collapse of Germany and hoping to spare her people further suffering, had requested that the advance to Rotterdam and Amsterdam be temporarily ceased. With the consolidation of this front the Crocs were released. Moving back east through Zutphen they now took the long road back into Germany, concentrating on the evening of the 23rd in a miserable wood just north of Meppen with the object of relieving 'C' Squadron, heading towards Emden with the Canadians. But the war on this front had virtually ceased and warning orders now came in to join British Second Army. Bremen, Hamburg, Denmark ? None of them—the whole thing was caving in and move after move was cancelled.

The war was fizzling out for the Playboys—fizzling out in the rain and mud of that miserable forest near Meppen, in deadly boredom in the leaking bivouacs, listening only to the rumours and counter-rumours of the endless news bulletins. And when the final news did come out it was all too prosaic. It was typical perhaps of this fantastic campaign that the greatest moment of all should fall so flat—it had been too long expected and that is the worst of inside dope. But somehow that evening the memory of those that had died seemed stronger. There was a nostalgia, a slight choking feeling—some of us had woken at last from a bad dream, but some of it remained so irrevocably real and true.

EPILOGUE

It was not until the 21st August 1945 that the Playboys said farewell to the veteran Crocs, handed them over to the regular 3 R.T.R. and moved into a desultory occupation role near Friedrichstadt. Only two command tanks, old and battle-scarred, had survived the whole campaign. The drafts had started and the Playboys were going off—civvy street, S.E.A.C., Regular Batalions.

But the story of the Playboys really ends on V.E. Day, May 8th. Though still in uniform from that day they would always be what they had originally been, Englishmen and citizens. What in fact they had always been—and therein perhaps is the real key to their strength and the glory of their achievements. For though the Army may claim the Englishman he remains above everything a righteous citizen in arms, and as such he triumphs over the mere militarist.

The story ends but the melody will for ever linger on. No more, no less, than millions of others the Playboys in the world's crucial hour of suffering and tribulation gave of their best, to the supreme sacrifice. Tough, noble, generous, laughing at the odds. I, the writer, pay tribute to the greatest bunch of guys I ever knew.

John Dean, Roland Beechey, Peter Sander, Freddie Roberts, Ginger Deverson, Tom Vernon—the long, long line of heroes and the far-off echo of the blazing guns. For us—

> They shall not grow old,
> As we that are left grow old,
> Age shall not weary them nor the years condemn,
> At the going down of the sun,
> And in the morning,
> We shall remember them.

ROLL OF HONOUR

KILLED IN ACTION

Lieut. R. C. Brooke	27 June, 1944
Tpr. H. Dady	27 June, 1944
Tpr. B. Woodcock	27 June, 1944
Capt. J. H. Dean	8 July, 1944
Lieut. R. H. Beechey	8 July, 1944
Cpl. F. Roberts	8 July, 1944
Tpr. C. Pitt	8 July, 1944
Sgt. S. Pipkin	18 July, 1944
L/Cpl. P. Murray	18 July, 1944
Tpr. S. Williams	18 July, 1945
L/Sgt. T. Vernon	18 July. 1944
Tpr. H. Deverson	18 July, 1944
Tpr. G. Jones	18 July, 1944
Tpr. B. Watts	18 July. 1944
Tpr. J. Humphrey	8 Aug., 1944
L/Cpl. D. Moore	14 Sept., 1944
Tpr, A. Frudd	14 Sept., 1944
Tpr. E. Guy	14 Sept., 1944
Lieut. P. C. F. Sander	24 Jan., 1945
Tpr. A. Uff	8 Mar., 1945
L/Cpl. A. Lewis	8 Mar., 1945

ROLL OF HONOUR

WOUNDED

Cpl. W. Marsden
Lieut. A. M. Beck
Cpl. E. Simpson
Tpr. G. Christieson
Tpr. R. Hands
Cpl D. Hischier
Cpl. C. Vine
Tpr. W. Halley
Tpr. J. Butterworth
Tpr. J. Smith
Tpr. G. Gregg
Major S. A. Spearpoint
Lieut. M. W. Henderson
Sgt. C. Douse
Sgt. C. Rowe
L/Cpl. H. Mulvaney
L/Cpl. J. Rispin
Tpr. S. Simler
Capt. R. R. Moss
Tpr. A. Cross
Major I. N. Ryle
Cpl. E. Phillips
Tpr. M. Emm
Tpr. O. Smith
Sgt. H. Bullard
Sgt. S. Driver
2/Lieut. G. C. Crowe

Tpr. S. Hartfield
Tpr. K. McDougall
Tpr. A. Fossey
Tpr. H. Millard
Sgt. G. Wetherell
Cpl. E. Grant
Cpl. W. Wallace
Tpr. R. Bewsher
Tpr. T. Walsh
2/Lieut. N. L. Hare
Sgt. L. Morley
L/Sgt. A. Cowe
L/Cpl. J. Rayman
Tpr. H. Adams
Tpr. T. Parry
Tpr. P. Thorne
Tpr. L. Worthy
Lieut. F. Philpot
Lieut. C. Shone
Lieut. H. A. Ward
L/Cpl. A. Allen
Tpr. T. Mills
Sgt. F. May
Tpr. J. Martin
Tpr. J. Moore
Tpr. B. Molyneux